ISBN: 978-0-7710-0317-2

Library and Archives Canada Cataloguing in Publication is available upon request

Published simultaneously in the United States of America by McClelland & Stewart, a division of Penguin Random House LLC, a Penguin Random House Company.

Library of Congress Control Number is available upon request

Printed and bound in the United States of America

McClelland & Stewart,
a division of Penguin Random House Canada Limited,
a Penguin Random House Company
www.penguinrandomhouse.ca

1   2   3   4   5   20   19   18   17   16

McClelland & Stewart

CONTENTS

INTRODUCTION

THE WAIT IS OVER

When the Cubs secured the final out of the 2016 World Series, the city of Chicago collectively exhaled; the so-called "Billy Goat Hex" had finally come to an end. Chicago's National League franchise ended a championship drought more than a century long in thrilling fashion, rallying from a 3-games-to-1 deficit against the Cleveland Indians to win the Fall Classic in Game 7 at Progressive Field.

Chicago's regular-season campaign was dominant: The club won a Major League—best 103 games and led the NL Central wire to wire. But when the postseason began, the Cubs had to overcome the Giants' even year magic and defeat a Clayton Kershaw-led Dodgers squad simply to reach the World Series. But with their eyes fixed on the ultimate prize, the Cubbies accomplished these feats and more, triumphing in three straight win-or-go-home games against the Indians to give their fanbase its first title since 1908.

The Cubs ultimately were able to climb to the top of the baseball world thanks to a stable of young talent. All five of Chicago's starting pitchers posted double-digits in wins during the regular season, while Kyle Hendricks led the Majors in ERA and ranked second in WHIP with Jon Lester not far behind in either category. Meanwhile, a core bolstered by Kris Bryant, Addison Russell, Anthony Rizzo, Javier Baez and countless other stars helped snap the franchise's winless streak, ushering in a new era of prosperity.

CHAMPIONS

THE WAIT IS OVER

THE CUBS BEGAN THE WORLD SERIES ON THE ROAD, AS CLEVELAND HOSTED GAME 1 OF THE WORLD SERIES (TOP) FOR THE FIRST TIME IN FRANCHISE HISTORY. AFTER CHICAGO DROPPED THE FIRST GAME, JAKE ARRIETA (BOTTOM) FIRED 5.2 INNINGS OF ONE-RUN BALL IN GAME 2 TO EVEN THE SERIES AS IT HEADED TO THE WINDY CITY.

AT JUST 24 AND 27 YEARS OLD, RESPECTIVELY, SLUGGERS KRIS BRYANT AND ANTHONY RIZZO DOMINATED IN THEIR FIRST WORLD SERIES. EACH HALF OF THE "BRYZZO" DUO WENT DEEP IN GAME 6 AT PROGRESSIVE FIELD.

THE WAIT IS OVER

(CLOCKWISE FROM TOP LEFT) WHEN THE CUBS RETURNED TO CHICAGO, THE PARTY STARTED, AS FANS PACKED WRIGLEYVILLE JUST TO BE A PART OF THE WORLD SERIES ATMOSPHERE. JUSTIN GRIMM CAME ON IN RELIEF OF KYLE HENDRICKS IN THE FIFTH INNING OF GAME 3 AND INDUCED A DOUBLE PLAY TO KEEP THE CONTEST SCORELESS, BUT THE CUBS WOULD ULTIMATELY LOSE, 1-0. ADDISON RUSSELL COLLECTED A NINTH-INNING HIT IN GAME 4, ONE OF HIS FOUR BASE KNOCKS IN THE SERIES' FIRST FIVE GAMES.

(CLOCKWISE FROM TOP LEFT) DEXTER FOWLER GAVE CUBS FANS HOPE AFTER KNOCKING A LEADOFF DOUBLE AND A SOLO HOMER IN GAME 4. THE NEXT NIGHT, THE TEAM DELIVERED, AS KRIS BRYANT SLUGGED A SOLO SHOT TO PUT CHICAGO ON THE BOARD AND AROLDIS CHAPMAN FIRED 2.2 SCORELESS INNINGS TO SECURE A 3-2 VICTORY.

THE WAIT IS OVER

WITH THE WORLD SERIES IN CHICAGO FOR THE FIRST TIME IN SEVEN-PLUS DECADES, FANS ALL AROUND THE CITY CAME OUT TO SHOW THEIR SUPPORT. MORE THAN 125,000 DIE-HARDS FLOODED THE FRIENDLY CONFINES DURING GAMES 3–5, AND PLENTY OTHERS GATHERED OUTSIDE THE STADIUM AND ON NEARBY ROOFTOPS.

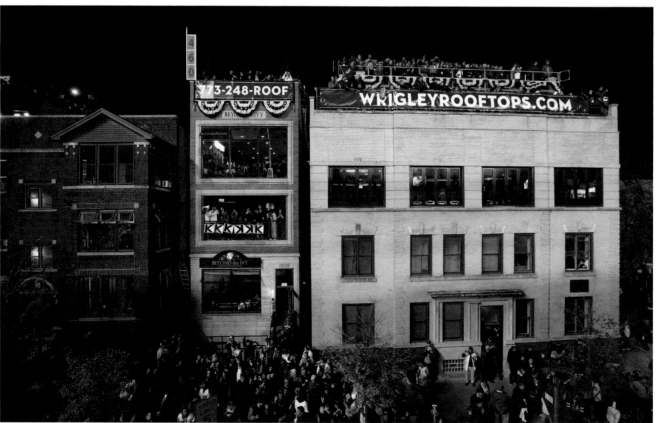

THE WAIT IS OVER

BILL MURRAY (TOP) WAS AMONG THE CONTINGENT OF CUBS FANS WHO JOURNEYED TO CLEVELAND WHEN THE SERIES FLIPPED TO GAME 6. THE CUBS DIDN'T LET THEIR ROAD TEAM STATUS FAZE THEM, THOUGH, AS ADDISON RUSSELL (LEFT) SMASHED THE FIRST WORLD SERIES GRAND SLAM SINCE 2005, WHILE ANTHONY RIZZO (ABOVE, LEFT) AND BEN ZOBRIST COMBINED FOR FIVE HITS AND FIVE RUNS IN CHICAGO'S 9-3 ROMP.

KRIS BRYANT (ABOVE) MADE THE THROW TO FIRST FOR THE FINAL OUT OF THE GAME.
AFTER COMING BACK FROM A 3-GAMES-TO-1 DEFICIT, THE TIGHT-KNIT PACK
CELEBRATED ITS WORLD SERIES TITLE.

THE WAIT IS OVER

CUBS FANS (TOP)
REJOICED, REVELING IN
THE TEAM'S FIRST
WORLD SERIES WIN
SINCE 1908. AFTER THE
GAME, ANTHONY RIZZO
HUGGED JON LESTER
(BELOW) IN
CELEBRATION.

WRIGLEY FIELD

A one-of-a-kind paean to a bygone era of baseball, Wrigley Field is the oldest and most beloved ballpark in the National League. And, fittingly, in the Cubs' 100th season within the Friendly Confines, it is now home to a long-awaited champion.

Whether it be the plethora of day games, the outfield ivy or the fans watching games from rooftops across the street, things have always been done just a bit differently on the North Side of Chicago since Wrigley's construction in 1914. The Cubbies moved in two years later, and baseball fans have flocked to the corner of Clark and Addison in Chicago's aptly-dubbed Wrigleyville neighborhood ever since.

In fact, it was Wrigley Field (with an assist from old Comiskey Park) that gave baseball one of its most cherished traditions in the singing of "Take Me Out to the Ball Game" during the seventh-inning stretch. Venerated broadcaster Harry Caray started the practice with the White Sox in the 1970s and brought it with him across town when he joined the Cubs in 1982. From there, it spread throughout the Majors.

Wrigley's famous bleachers, meanwhile, have given rise to another hallowed North Side tradition: throwing opponents' home run balls back onto the field. This practice, too, spread to other parks, but the Bleacher Bums popularized it, to the point where many savvy fans now carry a decoy around with them — just in case Kris Bryant happens to blast one their way.

CUBS EXECUTIVE BILL VEECK IS CREDITED WITH THE IDEA TO PLANT THE ICONIC IVY THAT HAS ADORNED THE OUTFIELD WALLS AT WRIGLEY FIELD SINCE 1937.

2016 SEASON IN REVIEW

Something about the 2016 season evoked a sense of nostalgia, especially for the most die-hard baseball fans. Maybe it was coming to grips with the conclusion of some historic careers many hoped would never end — we're looking at you, David Ortiz and Vin Scully — or mourning one that was cut far too short. Maybe it was witnessing Ken Griffey Jr. hold back tears during an emotional Hall of Fame speech. Whatever it was, 2016 also brought with it a remarkable amount of firsts and one-of-a-kind moments. It's this element of the unknown that keeps us coming back and wanting more, something that our national pastime delivers year in and year out.

As we say so long to some of the game's biggest stars, in comes a new crop with the chance to be better than the last. Ted Williams was once asked about how baseball would change after he stopped playing. "Baseball's future?" he responded, "Bigger and bigger, better and better! No question about it." These moments from 2016 prove that Williams' words ring true with each season that passes.

APRIL

SIZZLING START

Jake Arrieta, the 2015 National League Cy Young Award winner, picked up right where he left off in '16. The ace posted a 1.00 ERA and won all of his five starts in April, allowing just four total runs over 36 innings. Arrieta's crowning moment, however, came on April 21, when he twirled his second career no-hitter, this one against the Cincinnati Reds. In fact, he notched the second no-no a mere 10 starts after throwing his first, marking the third-fewest starts between no-hit bids in MLB history. Not surprisingly, thanks to Arrieta's efforts, the Cubs finished April with a 17-5 record, tying a franchise record.

SEASON IN REVIEW

AN UNLIKELY STORY

On April 6, **Trevor Story**, a 2011 first-round pick for the Rockies, became the first player in Major League history to homer in each of his first three games. He added two more shots to his total the following game.

IT'S IN THE CARDS

The Cardinals became the first team in history to collect three pinch-hit homers in a single game, as Jeremy Hazelbaker, Aledmys Diaz and **Greg Garcia** each went yard on April 8.

JAKE OF ALL TRADES

In a 16-0 victory over the Reds on April 21, **Jake Arrieta** sealed his second career no-hitter, becoming the third Cubs pitcher to throw multiple no-nos. The ace even helped his own cause at the plate, also becoming the third Cubs pitcher to have two hits in his own no-hit bid, joining Sam Jones (1955) and Walter Thornton (1898).

MAY

THE COMPLETE PACKAGE

Heading into the 2016 season, **Kyle Hendricks** projected to be a useful piece at the back end of a strong starting rotation. These early expectations were obliterated as he quickly put together a sparkling, Cy Young Award–worthy season. May 28 could be considered the turning point of his season, as the lanky right-hander tossed his second career complete game, holding the Phillies to just one run over nine innings that day. Throughout the remainder of the season, he would allow fewer than three runs in all but three more starts. His already impressive 2.93 ERA continued to plummet, and he would finish the season with a league-best 2.13 mark.

SEASON IN REVIEW

WALK THAT WAY

Bryce Harper drew six walks in a May 8 contest against the Cubs to tie the MLB record. The Nationals superstar also recorded a hit-by-pitch.

MOTOR CITY MILESTONE

Justin Verlander fanned Twins batter Eddie Rosario on May 18 to notch his 2,000th career strikeout in a 6-3 win over Minnesota. The Tigers' ace enjoyed a resurgent 2016 season, whiffing more than a batter per inning and posting his lowest ERA since 2012.

MAX EFFORT

On May 11, **Max Scherzer** took the mound against his former team and mowed down Detroit's potent offense, tying a Major League record with 20 strikeouts. He became just the fourth pitcher in MLB history to do so in nine innings, joining Roger Clemens — who did so twice — Kerry Wood and Randy Johnson.

2 0 1 6
WORLD SERIES
CHAMPIONS

SEASON IN REVIEW

JUNE

SPRING AWAKENING

First baseman **Anthony Rizzo** slugged 30-plus home runs for the third straight season in 2016, and more than a quarter of those longballs came in the month of June. During an impressive 25-game stretch, he posted a 1.212 OPS and a .378 average, and hit safely in all but three contests during the month. He knocked 21 RBI to go along with eight home runs, logged nine multi-hit outings and a month later earned a National League All-Star nod for the third straight season as a result.

SEASON IN REVIEW

ROOKIE SENSATION

Michael Fulmer gave up a run for the first time in 33.1 innings on June 17, ending the longest scoreless streak by a rookie starting pitcher since Fernando Valenzuela's in 1981. It was the only run he would allow in the outing.

DESIGNATED PITCHER

On June 30, the Giants played the A's across the bay at Oakland Coliseum, where Manager Bruce Bochy chose to forego a DH — the first time that's happened since 1976. He instead let his starting pitcher, **Madison Bumgarner**, hit for himself, and the ace rewarded his skipper by knocking a double in the third inning and scoring a run.

THE SOARING O's

Baltimore's **Hyun Soo Kim** swatted a solo homer on June 30, the final day of the month, giving the Orioles the all-time team record for longballs hit in June (56).

JULY

FIREBALLER

In an attempt to shore up an already solid bullpen, the Cubs acquired the league's hardest thrower, and arguably its most electric reliever, from the Yankees just before the trade deadline. **Aroldis Chapman** notched his first save for the Cubs on July 27, striking out two of the three batters he faced, a fact that soon became all-too familiar for opponents. Averaging nearly 101 mph with his fastball, Chapman converted 15 saves down the stretch and allowed just three earned runs in the ensuing 25.2 innings. He would finish the season with more than 30 saves for the fifth straight time and an ERA below 2.00 for the third time in his career.

MARATHON MATCHUP

On July 1, the Indians opened the month by beating the Blue Jays in a six-hour affair when **Carlos Santana** swatted a solo homer in the top of the 19th. The victory marked Cleveland's franchise-record 14th-straight victory.

STAR-STUDDED

San Diego's Petco Park hosted 2016 All-Star Week, including the All-Star Game presented by MasterCard and the T-Mobile Home Run Derby. **Giancarlo Stanton** dominated the Derby, swatting 18 of the 19 longest homers in the event en route to his first crown. In the Midsummer Classic, the AL gave **David Ortiz** a fitting send-off, winning the game, 4-2, as Big Papi received a standing ovation in his final All-Star at-bat.

AUGUST

SWEET SUMMER SLUGGER

On August 26, **Kris Bryant** swatted two home runs against the Dodgers, the second of which was a go-ahead shot in the 10th inning that lifted the Cubs to a 6–4 victory. Yet the incredible showing is par for the course for last season's NL Rookie of the Year. Chicago's third baseman hit 39 home runs, scored 121 runs and notched 102 RBI in his sophomore campaign, all while maintaining a .292 average. He took Player of the Month honors in August after crushing 10 homers, plating 22 runs and scoring 29 times, all while posting a 1.220 OPS. He even knocked three or more hits three times, including a 5-for-5 effort against Milwaukee on August 18. Thanks in large part to Bryant's sizzling bat, the Cubs posted a 22-6 record that month, and it became hard to hear his walk-up music over the M-V-P chants from the crowd as the calendar turned to September.

MR. 3,000

After a long, historic pursuit, **Ichiro Suzuki** knocked a triple on August 7 for his 3,000th Major League hit to become the 30th member of the exclusive club. Earlier in the season, he notched hit No. 2,979 in the Big Leagues, which, combined with the 1,278 knocks he had in Japan, helped him to unofficially top Pete Rose's 4,256 mark.

A TORONTO TRADITION

Josh Donaldson swatted three home runs on August 28 in a game against the Twins to propel the Blue Jays to a win. Fans at Rogers Centre tossed hats onto the field to celebrate MLB's version of a "hat trick."

GREAT BRITTON

On August 24, Baltimore closer **Zach Britton** allowed his first earned run after notching 43 consecutive scoreless appearances, the longest streak of its kind since the earned run became an official stat. He would finish the season with 47 saves and an ERA and WHIP well below 1.00.

SEPTEMBER

LOCKDOWN LEFTY

Was any pitcher in the league better than **Jon Lester** in September? Probably not. The crafty southpaw elevated his game to a whole new level come autumn, as he allowed just two runs over 37.2 innings of work in the month. He fired a complete game in a 2-1 win over the Cubs' eventual NLDS adversary San Francisco Giants on September 2 and never looked back, notching five of his 10 straight wins and posting an otherworldly 0.48 ERA to win the NL Pitcher of the Month Award. In his second season with the Cubs, the veteran finished with the second-lowest ERA (2.44) of his career and the lowest WHIP (1.02).

SEASON IN REVIEW

2B OR NOT 2B

The Twins' **Brian Dozier** hit a game-tying homer on September 22, his 42nd of the season and 40th in a game that he was playing second base — a mark that broke the AL record.

A VERY PLEASANT GOODBYE

On September 25, legendary broadcaster **Vin Scully** called his last Dodgers home game after working for a record 67 seasons. The team authored a fitting finish, as Charlie Culberson clocked a walk-off, game-winning homer in the bottom of the 10th and Los Angeles clinched the NL West.

STRIKEOUT SURGE

Cubs starter **Kyle Hendricks** fanned Pirates catcher Francisco Cervelli in the second inning of his team's game on September 26, tallying the 37,447th strikeout of the 2016 season. At that point, it was the highest total in history, and it only continued to climb.

MARLINS PITCHER FERNANDEZ, WHO WAS BELOVED AROUND THE GAME, TRAGICALLY PASSED AWAY IN LATE SEPTEMBER AT JUST 24 YEARS OLD.

BIGGER THAN BASEBALL

A review of the 2016 campaign would be incomplete without acknowledging a late-season tragedy. Jose Fernandez represented all that is great about baseball on and off the field. The Marlins' Cuba-born ace died in a boating accident off the coast of Miami on September 25, but his legacy is bigger even than his accomplishments on the mound.

That's not to say that the numbers were anything short of phenomenal. After debuting in 2013 at just 20 years old, Fernandez won the NL Rookie of the Year Award. This past July, he also became the fastest starting pitcher in terms of innings pitched and batters faced to record 500 career strikeouts.

And yet, for a player of his talent, he will best be remembered for his honest, jubilant personality — and the boyish grin he always sported. He'd sometimes dance in the dugout or talk to the batter from the mound. One night, after securing a win in L.A., he pulled up a chair and watched a post-game fireworks show from the field. The baseball world couldn't help but get caught up in his pure, unadulterated love of the game.

"Jose was one of the special cases who we all enjoyed," said David Ortiz. "The most important thing was his kindness, the kind of person he was."

The Marlins honored Fernandez in an emotional ceremony before playing the Mets on September 26, and every member of the team wore his No.16 during the contest, their first without the beloved ace. Miami also retired the number, making it the only retired number in franchise history, excepting Jackie Robinson's league-wide No. 42.

If the 24-year-old taught us anything, it is that his passion for baseball and life itself is a quality that deserves to be remembered, emulated and celebrated.

SEASON IN REVIEW

FINAL 2016 STANDINGS

AMERICAN LEAGUE

EAST	W	L	GB
xBoston	93	69	–
wBaltimore	89	73	4.0
wToronto	89	73	4.0
New York	84	78	9.0
Tampa Bay	68	94	25.0

CENTRAL	W	L	GB
xCleveland	94	67	–
Detroit	86	75	8.0
Kansas City	81	81	13.5
Chicago	78	84	16.5
Minnesota	59	103	35.5

WEST	W	L	GB
xTexas	95	67	–
Seattle	86	76	9.0
Houston	84	78	11.0
Los Angeles	74	88	21.0
Oakland	69	93	26.0

NATIONAL LEAGUE

EAST	W	L	GB
xWashington	95	67	–
wNew York	87	75	8.0
Miami	79	82	15.5
Philadelphia	71	91	24.0
Atlanta	68	93	26.5

CENTRAL	W	L	GB
xChicago*	103	58	–
St. Louis	86	76	17.5
Pittsburgh*	78	83	25.0
Milwaukee	73	89	30.5
Cincinnati	68	94	35.5

WEST	W	L	GB
xLos Angeles	91	71	–
wSan Francisco	87	75	4.0
Colorado	75	87	16.0
Arizona	69	93	22.0
San Diego	68	94	23.0

*x Division winner; w Wild Card; *Also recorded a tie Game*

CATEGORY LEADERS

AMERICAN LEAGUE

Batting Average	Jose Altuve, Houston	.338
Hits	Jose Altuve, Houston	216
Home Runs	Mark Trumbo, Baltimore	47
RBI	Edwin Encarnacion, Toronto David Ortiz, Boston	127
Stolen Bases	Rajai Davis, Cleveland	43
Wins	Rick Porcello, Boston	22
ERA	Aaron Sanchez, Toronto	3.00
Strikeouts	Justin Verlander, Detroit	254
Saves	Zach Britton, Baltimore	47

NATIONAL LEAGUE

Batting Average	DJ LeMahieu, Colorado	.348
Hits	Jean Segura, Arizona	203
Home Runs	Nolan Arenado, Colorado Chris Carter, Milwaukee	41
RBI	Nolan Arenado, Colorado	133
Stolen Bases	Jonathan Villar, Milwaukee	62
Wins	Max Scherzer, Washington	20
ERA	Kyle Hendricks, Chicago	2.13
Strikeouts	Max Scherzer, Washington	284
Saves	Jeurys Familia, New York	51

NATIONAL LEAGUE DIVISION SERIES

GAME 1, OCTOBER 7
CHICAGO 1, SAN FRANCISCO 0

How well did things go for the Cubs in Game 1 of the NLDS? So well that it was Javier Baez, who'd been inserted into the lineup for his defense, who provided all the offensive spark needed to defeat the Giants when he launched a full-count fastball from Johnny Cueto into the basket rimming the left-field bleachers at Wrigley Field. Cueto had followed Madison Bumgarner's example from the Wild Card Game and threw 7.1 scoreless innings before Baez ended the shutout.

Jon Lester, in his fourth straight year in the playoffs, served up a leadoff single in each of the first three innings but then kept the Giants' bats at bay and departed after firing eight shutout innings of his own, striking out five. Cubs closer Aroldis Chapman pitched a scoreless ninth for the save. "It was a classic, kind of an old-school baseball game," Chicago manager Joe Maddon said. "Obviously, you like to win those things, but give both teams credit. That was a really well-played game of baseball."

	1	2	3	4	5	6	7	8	9	R	H	E
SAN FRANCISCO	0	0	0	0	0	0	0	0	0	0	6	0
CHICAGO	0	0	0	0	0	0	0	1	X	1	3	0

WP: Lester LP: Cueto SV: Chapman
HR: CHC: Baez

HEADING INTO THE NLDS, THE GIANTS WERE FRESH OFF A VICTORY IN THE WILD CARD GAME, IN WHICH THEY DEFEATED THE NEW YORK METS. THE CUBS, MEANWHILE, ENTERED THE POSTSEASON AFTER SECURING MORE THAN 100 REGULAR-SEASON WINS.

POSTSEASON VETERAN LESTER SHUT DOWN THE GIANTS' OFFENSE FOR EIGHT INNINGS TO NOTCH THE VICTORY IN GAME 1 OF THE NLDS.

"Cueto threw the heck out of the ball. I kind of figured as we got going it would come down to one mistake, and luckily we didn't make one and they did. And I think that's just the beginning of the series. I think we're going to be in for it and it's going to be a grind, and we'll show up tomorrow and try to do it again."

Jon Lester

NL DIVISION SERIES

BAEZ WAS THE HERO IN THE OPENING GAME OF THE DIVISION SERIES, LAUNCHING A SOLO HOMER WITH ONE OUT IN THE EIGHTH TO GIVE THE CUBS ALL THE RUN SUPPORT THEY NEEDED FOR A VICTORY.

CUETO (RIGHT) FIRED 7.1 SCORELESS INNINGS, BUT WAS SADDLED WITH A TOUGH-LUCK LOSS AFTER ALLOWING A SOLO HOMER. CHAPMAN ENTERED THE GAME IN RELIEF OF LESTER AND SHUT THE DOOR.

GAME 2, OCTOBER 8
CHICAGO 5, SAN FRANCISCO 2

To beat the Giants in Game 2, all the Cubs needed was for their pitchers to hit. Kyle Hendricks, MLB's regular-season ERA leader, smacked a two-run single in the contest, and Travis Wood added a solo home run to lift the Cubs to a 5-2 victory over the Giants in front of an excited crowd at Wrigley Field.

"Now we go to San Francisco, and we're going to play for one more win," said Cubs closer Aroldis Chapman, who picked up his second consecutive save with a two-strikeout, 1-2-3 ninth inning.

Hendricks had to leave the game with two outs in the fourth after a line drive off the bat of Angel Pagan hit him in the right forearm. The scorcher had an exit velocity of 94 mph according to Statcast, but X-rays were negative. Wood

replaced Hendricks, and in the bottom of the inning crushed his 10th career home run to cement a 5-2 lead.

San Francisco starter Jeff Samardzija also exited early, but for different reasons. The right-hander, who pitched for the Cubs from 2008-14, was knocked out of the game after serving up four runs on six hits over two innings.

	1	2	3	4	5	6	7	8	9	R	H	E
SAN FRANCISCO	0	0	2	0	0	0	0	0	0	2	6	1
CHICAGO	1	3	0	1	0	0	0	0	X	5	9	3

WP: Wood **LP:** Samardzija **SV:** Chapman
HR: CHC: Wood

HENDRICKS HELPED HIS OWN CAUSE WITH A TWO-RUN SINGLE BEFORE EXITING THE GAME AFTER GETTING HIT BY A LINE DRIVE.

"As a bullpen guy you're always prepared, especially with Joe [Maddon], for any situation. So I was ready to come in. And then the at-bat, I figured he was probably going to start me out with a cutter and I made a good swing on it and was fortunate enough to hit it out of the park."

Travis Wood

WOOD BECAME THE FIRST RELIEF PITCHER SINCE 1924 TO HIT A HOME RUN IN THE POSTSEASON. HIS BLAST IN THE FOURTH INNING HELPED THE CUBS TAKE A 2-GAMES-TO-NONE SERIES LEAD INTO SAN FRANCISCO.

GAME 3, OCTOBER 10
SAN FRANCISCO 6, CHICAGO 5

Despite being in enemy territory, the Cubs jumped ahead early thanks to starter Jake Arrieta's three-run, second-inning homer off Madison Bumgarner. The blast ended Bumgarner's postseason scoreless streak at 24 consecutive innings, matching Lew Burdette for the third-longest ever. But in a back-and-forth affair, Joe Panik ultimately plated Brandon Crawford with a double in the 13th inning to lift the Giants to a 6-5 victory at home.

Chicago had erased the Giants' 5-3 edge in the ninth on Kris Bryant's two-run shot off Sergio Romo, which sent the game into extras. But Crawford led off the 13th inning with a double off Mike Montgomery, who was pitching his fifth inning of relief. Then up came Panik, whose drive caromed off the right-field wall as Crawford raced home, sending fans at AT&T Park home happy.

Panik's knock ended a five-hour, four-minute game that was just 29 minutes shy of the total time taken to play the first *two* games at Wrigley Field. It was the longest playoff game in Cubs history, topping the 12-inning Game 6 of the 1945 World Series. "This is October baseball," Arrieta said. "We know games are going to be very closely contested."

San Francisco, which won the World Series in 2010, '12 and '14, recorded its 10th consecutive victory when facing postseason elimination.

	1	2	3	4	5	6	7	8	9	10	11	12	13	R	H	E
CHICAGO	0	3	0	0	0	0	0	0	2	0	0	0	0	5	10	2
SAN FRANCISCO	0	0	1	0	1	0	0	3	0	0	0	0	1	6	13	1

WP: Blach **LP:** Montgomery
HR: CHC: Arrieta, Bryant

ARRIETA WENT TOE-TO-TOE WITH FELLOW ACE BUMGARNER. IN ADDITION TO THROWING SIX INNINGS OF TWO-RUN BALL, HE BLASTED A THREE-RUN HOMER.

PANIK (LEFT) WALKED TWICE IN GAME 3 BEFORE COLLECTING A WALK-OFF DOUBLE IN THE BOTTOM OF THE 13TH. BRYANT ALSO HAD A DOUBLE AND A HOME RUN, BUT IT ULTIMATELY WASN'T ENOUGH FOR THE CUBS.

"Good baseball game. That's my takeaway. I think that both sides should be somewhat exhilarated. Obviously they win, so they're going to feel a bit better about it, but there's nothing on our side to be ashamed of. I was really proud of our kids."

Cubs Manager Joe Maddon

GAME 4, OCTOBER 11
CHICAGO 6, SAN FRANCISCO 5

After every game, the Cubs' mantra was "We never quit." They yelled it together, like a college cheer, and repeated it time and again. In Game 4, that attitude carried the Cubs into the NLCS for the second straight year, and they got there by toppling a team dubbed the "October Giant." After being shut down by Matt Moore for eight innings, the Cubs rallied against San Francisco's beleaguered bullpen for a historic four-run ninth inning and posted a 6-5 victory over the Giants to take the best-of-five series, 3-games-to-1.

The Cubs' comeback was the biggest to clinch a series in postseason history. In erasing a three-run deficit against five different relievers, Chicago matched the Mets' feat in the ninth inning of Game 6 of the 1986 NLCS. With his team trailing, 5-2, in the ninth, Kris Bryant led off with a single. Anthony Rizzo then walked, and Ben Zobrist followed with an RBI double. Willson Contreras then smacked a two-run single to tie the score at 5-5, and Javier Baez delivered an RBI single for the game-winner. Aroldis Chapman picked up his third save in four games, and the victory party started at AT&T Park.

	1	2	3	4	5	6	7	8	9	R	H	E
CHICAGO	0	0	1	0	1	0	0	0	4	6	6	0
SAN FRANCISCO	1	0	0	2	2	0	0	0	0	5	11	2

WP: Rondon **LP:** Smith **SV:** Chapman
HR: CHC: Ross

THE CUBS SECURED THE FRANCHISE'S SECOND STRAIGHT TRIP TO THE NLCS. THIS TIME, THEY CLINCHED ON THE ROAD IN SAN FRANCISCO AND CELEBRATED WITH THE NORTH SIDE CONTINGENT THAT TRAVELED TO SUPPORT THEM.

AFTER THE CUBS RALLIED FOR FOUR RUNS IN THE TOP OF THE NINTH, CHAPMAN NOTCHED HIS THIRD SAVE OF THE SERIES TO SEND CHICAGO TO THE NEXT ROUND.

"I wasn't worried; it's just that we weren't ourselves for eight innings. We weren't having the kind of at-bats we normally have.... Hitting before the ninth inning is overrated anyway. It's about doing it when it matters, I guess."

Cubs President Theo Epstein

BAEZ ONCE AGAIN PLAYED A KEY ROLE IN THE VICTORY, DELIVERING A GO-AHEAD SINGLE IN THE TOP OF THE NINTH TO CLINCH THE SERIES.

2016 WORLD SERIES CHAMPIONS

NL DIVISION SERIES

VETERAN JOHN LACKEY STARTED THE GAME FOR THE CUBS AND STRUCK OUT FOUR GIANTS OVER FOUR INNINGS, BUT DIDN'T RECEIVE A DECISION.

NATIONAL LEAGUE CHAMPIONSHIP SERIES

GAME 1, OCTOBER 15
CHICAGO 8, LOS ANGELES 4

In Game 1 of the NLCS, the Cubs found another late-inning spark, as they seem to have all postseason. This time the hero was Miguel Montero, who smacked a grand slam with two outs in the eighth to power the Cubs to an 8-4 victory.

The Cubs led, 3-1, after seven and called on Aroldis Chapman to keep it that way with the bases loaded and no outs in the eighth. Chapman had struggled with runners on in Game 3 of the NLDS and blew a save, but he fanned Corey Seager on a 101-mph fastball and got Yasiel Puig swinging at a 103-mph heater. Veteran Adrian Gonzalez was unfazed, though, lining a two-RBI single up the middle to tie the score.

But the Cubs answered in their half, as a Ben Zobrist double and two intentional walks set the table for Montero's slam, his first career postseason home run, to give Chicago a 7-3 lead. Dexter Fowler followed with a solo shot of his own.

Javier Baez, the NLDS hero, stretched a single into a double in the second inning and also stole home, becoming the first Cubs player to do so in the postseason since Jimmy Slagle in Game 4 of the 1907 World Series.

	1	2	3	4	5	6	7	8	9	R	H	E
LOS ANGELES	0	0	0	0	1	0	0	2	1	4	9	0
CHICAGO	1	2	0	0	0	0	0	5	X	8	9	0

WP: Chapman **LP:** Blanton

HR: LAD: Ethier CHC: Fowler, Montero

MORE THAN 42,000 CUBS DIE-HARDS PACKED THE FRIENDLY CONFINES FOR THE CUBS' SECOND NLCS APPEARANCE IN AS MANY YEARS. THOUSANDS MORE WHO COULDN'T FIT INTO THE BALLPARK FILLED WRIGLEYVILLE'S SURROUNDING STREETS.

ADDISON RUSSELL, WHO'S JUST 22, APPEARED IN THE PLAYOFFS WITH THE CUBS IN 2015 BUT DIDN'T PLAY IN THE NATIONAL LEAGUE CHAMPIONSHIP SERIES AGAINST THE METS. IN THE 2016 NLCS, HE WENT 6 FOR 22 WITH A PAIR OF HOME RUNS.

"As a kid, you always dream of these situations. That's what you live for. This one is special because it's in front of this special crowd that we have. It's a great sensation, and I'm going to keep searching to see if it gets even better."

Miguel Montero

THE DYNAMIC BAEZ (ABOVE) MANUFACTURED A RUN IN THE SECOND WHEN HE DOUBLED, TOOK THIRD ON A WILD PITCH AND STOLE HOME, GIVING CHICAGO A 3-0 LEAD. ALTHOUGH THE DODGERS WOULD TIE IT, MONTERO (OPPOSITE) BLASTED A GRAND SLAM TO PUT HIS CLUB UP AGAIN ON ITS WAY TO A VICTORY IN GAME 1 OF THE NLCS.

GAME 2, OCTOBER 16
LOS ANGELES 1, CHICAGO 0

Clayton Kershaw silenced the mighty Cubs when he took the mound at Wrigley Field, holding them to two hits over seven scoreless innings in a 1–0 win that tied the NLCS at one game apiece. Adrian Gonzalez supported his ace with a homer in the second off regular-season NL ERA leader Kyle Hendricks. With that longball, Gonzalez had gone deep in six consecutive postseason series, one shy of the Major League record, with three of the longballs providing go-ahead runs.

With no margin for error, Kershaw made the homer stand, but only barely, as Javier Baez launched a laser to the warning track in center field. Joc Pederson caught it to end the seventh, though, and Dodgers Manager Dave Roberts went right to Kenley Jansen for a six-out save, just three days after he threw 51 pitches to set up Kershaw's save in the NLDS clincher.

"To see how Kersh takes this team on his back, you want to go out there and give it the extra inch and try to get the win," said Jansen.

Over the course of the postseason, Kershaw had thrown 19.1 innings in three starts and one historic save, continuing to rewrite his October reputation. The only games the Dodgers had won to that point were those in which their ace pitched.

	1	2	3	4	5	6	7	8	9	R	H	E
LOS ANGELES	0	1	0	0	0	0	0	0	0	1	3	1
CHICAGO	0	0	0	0	0	0	0	0	0	0	2	0

WP: Kershaw **LP:** Hendricks **SV**: Jansen
HR: LAD: Gonzalez

HENDRICKS WAS SADDLED WITH A TOUGH LOSS AFTER GOING UP AGAINST KERSHAW. HE ALLOWED JUST ONE RUN, A GONZALEZ HOMER, BUT THAT PROVED TO BE THE DIFFERENCE.

"[Kershaw] didn't strike a lot of guys out. I was taking a little bit of solace in that. If we're moving the ball that much, you would think that we're going to get more hits than we did. He kept the ball off the fat part of our bats. He threw strikes like he normally does. So, despite not having rest, his command and velocity were still good."

Cubs Manager Joe Maddon

KERSHAW DIDN'T NECESSARILY HAVE STRIKEOUT STUFF — HE WHIFFED SIX CUBS BATTERS OVER SEVEN FRAMES — BUT HE HELD THE HOME TEAM TO JUST A PAIR OF HITS TO WALK AWAY WITH A 1-0 VICTORY.

GAME 3, OCTOBER 18
LOS ANGELES 6, CHICAGO 0

Yasmani Grandal and Justin Turner took Cubs starter Jake Arrieta deep, and Rich Hill silenced Chicago at the plate as the NLCS shifted to Dodger Stadium.

With the Dodgers' starting rotation short-handed and needing innings from Hill, the former Cubs lefty delivered six scoreless to outpitch Arrieta. Hill snapped curveball after curveball and allowed just a pair of singles to Kris Bryant in L.A.'s second straight shutout of the vaunted Cubs lineup.

Grandal, who hit .100 through his first 20 at-bats in this year's postseason, reappeared as the regular-season, 27-homer version of himself by rocketing a two-run shot with two outs in the fourth inning — a blast that had an exit velocity of 107.8 mph, according to Statcast. Turner later chased Arrieta by leading off the sixth inning with a longball that went out at 105 miles per hour. The blast marked the eighth straight postseason game in which a Dodgers player homered, matching the second-longest streak in Los Angeles franchise history.

Rookies combined for the Dodgers' first run in the third inning, the second of Corey Seager's three singles cashing in on a leadoff single by Andrew Toles.

	1	2	3	4	5	6	7	8	9	R	H	E
CHICAGO	0	0	0	0	0	0	0	0	0	0	4	0
LOS ANGELES	0	0	1	2	0	1	0	2	X	6	10	0

WP: Hill **LP:** Arrieta
HR: LAD: Grandal, Turner

BRYANT, WHO WENT 2 FOR 4 AT THE PLATE IN GAME 3 OF THE NLCS, BACKED UP ARRIETA (OPPOSITE, BOTTOM) ON DEFENSE. BUT THEIR EFFORTS WEREN'T ENOUGH IN A 6-0 LOSS IN WHICH HILL (OPPOSITE, TOP) STRUCK OUT SIX.

"You have to be able to push back mentally. Because when it comes down to work, you don't need any more batting practice or video study or data. We're just not hitting, so we're making it easier on their defense. It's more of a mental exercise than a physical one right now."

Cubs Manager Joe Maddon

GAME 4, OCTOBER 19
CHICAGO 10, LOS ANGELES 2

In Game 4, Addison Russell and Anthony Rizzo both broke out of slumps with home runs in a 10-2 blowout win at Dodger Stadium. The Cubs deadlocked the NLCS at two games apiece, fashioning the beginnings of their ultimate comeback.

The Cubs' offense, blanked for 21 consecutive innings, awoke against 20-year-old Dodgers rookie Julio Urias, the youngest pitcher ever to start a postseason game. Ben Zobrist's bunt single sparked a fourth-inning rally before Russell, who collected three hits on the night, homered to center to cap the four-run frame. Rizzo then went deep off Pedro Baez in the fifth inning and added a two-run single in a five-run sixth.

The Dodgers uncharacteristically helped beat themselves, committing four fielding errors — more than in any other game this year and the most in a Dodgers postseason game since the 1974 NLCS — and ending two innings when their runners were cut down on the bases. The pair of outs included a controversial review in the second inning when Adrian Gonzalez was thrown out at the plate; the call stood after Los Angeles challenged.

Mike Montgomery relieved starter John Lackey in the fifth, and picked up the victory. The Dodgers, meanwhile, collected their only pair runs when Justin Turner's possible double-play grounder deflected off Montgomery's glove into left field for a two-run single in the fifth.

	1	2	3	4	5	6	7	8	9	R	H	E
CHICAGO	0	0	0	4	1	5	0	0	0	10	13	2
LOS ANGELES	0	0	0	0	2	0	0	0	0	2	6	4

WP: Montgomery **LP:** Urias
HR: CHC: Rizzo, Russell

GONZALEZ THOUGHT HE SLID IN UNDER THE GLOVE OF WILLSON CONTRERAS, BUT REPLAY REVIEW RULED THAT HOME PLATE UMPIRE ANGEL HERNANDEZ'S OUT CALL STOOD.

ZOBRIST REACHED BASE ON AN INFIELD SINGLE IN THE FOURTH AND CAME AROUND TO SCORE THE FIRST RUN OF THE GAME, IN WHICH CHICAGO POSTED AN EVENTUAL EIGHT-RUN MARGIN OF VICTORY.

RUSSELL'S TWO-RUN, FOURTH-INNING HOMER (ABOVE) CAPPED THE CUBS' FOUR-RUN EXPLOSION THAT FRAME. THE STUD SHORTSTOP COLLECTED THREE HITS IN FIVE AT-BATS ON THE NIGHT. RIZZO (OPPOSITE) ALSO HOMERED, AND SCORED TWICE IN GAME 4 OF THE NLCS.

"Our confidence is up. The best part about the postseason is the next at-bat. You've got to turn the page to the next at-bat, and you've got to be ready for that big situation. All the guys in the clubhouse, all the veterans, are there telling you, 'It just takes one at-bat.' It's all about winning games, and we came up on the good side tonight."

Anthony Rizzo

GAME 5, OCTOBER 20
CHICAGO 8, LOS ANGELES 4

Since he took over as the Cubs' skipper, Joe Maddon downplayed the franchise's long championship drought, ignored any talk about curses, and focused on the present. But after an 8-4 victory over the Dodgers in Game 5 of the NLCS, the Cubs stared the World Series in its face, standing just one win away from their first appearance since 1945.

Addison Russell broke a 1-1 tie in the sixth inning with a home run (for the second consecutive game) — the third homer that reliever Joe Blanton allowed in the NLCS — as Jon Lester won his rematch with Kenta Maeda. The Cubs started fast against the Dodgers' hurler, as Dexter Fowler led off the game with a single and Anthony Rizzo followed with a one-out RBI double. Los Angeles, meanwhile, tied the game in the fourth when Howie Kendrick doubled and scored on Adrian Gonzalez's infield chopper. That was the only run that Lester would allow over seven innings, though, as the veteran notched his eighth career postseason victory.

The Cubs tacked on five runs (four unearned) in the eighth, highlighted by a three-run double by Javier Baez.

	1	2	3	4	5	6	7	8	9	R	H	E
CHICAGO	1	0	0	0	0	2	0	5	0	8	13	2
LOS ANGELES	0	0	0	1	0	0	0	1	2	4	9	1

WP: Lester **LP:** Blanton
HR: CHC: Russell

WITH THE CUBS UP, 5-1, IN THE EIGHTH, BAEZ DOUBLED IN THREE RUNS TO PROVIDE SOME VALUABLE INSURANCE FOR LESTER (OPPOSITE), WHO EXITED AFTER SEVEN STRONG FRAMES.

NL CHAMPIONSHIP SERIES

"I just get fired up getting outs. Obviously not a great way to start the game, with a walk. We can't allow free base runners. I was just happy to get out of that inning more than anything. I play this game with emotion."

Jon Lester

FOWLER, THE FIRST BATTER OF THE GAME, SINGLED OFF DODGERS STARTER MAEDA AND SCORED ON A DOUBLE JUST TWO BATTERS LATER.

RUSSELL (TOP) LAUNCHED A TWO-RUN HOMER IN THE SIXTH TO BREAK A 1–1 TIE AND ULTIMATELY CONTRIBUTED TO THE CUBS' THIRD WIN OF THE SERIES, SENDING THE FANS WHO SUPPORTED THEM AT DODGER STADIUM INTO A FRENZY.

GAME 6, OCTOBER 22
CHICAGO 5, LOS ANGELES 0

The Cubs punched their first ticket to the World Series since 1945 with a convincing 5-0 win in front of the Wrigley Field faithful in Game 6. Anthony Rizzo and Willson Contreras each belted solo home runs to back Kyle Hendricks — who outdueled Clayton Kershaw — and power the Cubs to their first National League pennant since 1945.

The team that scored first won each game in the series, and Chicago got off to a quick start in the home half of the first. Dexter Fowler, who boasted a career .409 average against the Dodgers' ace, doubled on the third pitch, and scored soon after on a Kris Bryant single. The third baseman would later cross the plate on Ben Zobrist's sacrifice fly.

Contreras led off the fourth inning with a home run to left. According to Statcast, the exit velocity was 105.5 mph, making the blast the third-hardest-hit homer off Kershaw this season. Rizzo didn't hit his as hard with two outs in the fifth, but it still landed in the right-field bleachers.

Aroldis Chapman came in to get a double play to end the eighth, and tossed a scoreless ninth to finish the game. Hendricks and the fireballer combined to face the minimum number of batters, sending the Cubs to the World Series.

	1	2	3	4	5	6	7	8	9	R	H	E
LOS ANGELES	0	0	0	0	0	0	0	0	0	0	2	1
CHICAGO	2	1	0	1	1	0	0	0	X	5	7	1

WP: Hendricks **LP:** Kershaw
HR: CHC: Contreras, Rizzo

WRIGLEY FIELD'S ICONIC MARQUEE PROUDLY BROADCAST ITS RESIDENTS' NATIONAL LEAGUE PENNANT AND WORLD SERIES BERTH FOLLOWING GAME 6 OF THE NLCS.

"I think the outside forces felt different. You felt the buzz around the stadium. It was loud in there. I hope [the fans] enjoy this. They have been waiting a long time for it. It's been our goal from day one. We're still not there yet. So as good as this feels, as much as we're going to enjoy it, getting up tomorrow, we know what we've got to do."

Kyle Hendricks

THE POWERFUL CUBS SQUAD GOT THE CHANCE TO CELEBRATE ITS PENNANT-CLINCHING VICTORY AT HOME, WHERE THE CLUB HAD POSTED A .704 WINNING PERCENTAGE DURING THE 2016 REGULAR SEASON.

"It was very special to me to be on the podium with Mr. Ricketts, Jed, Theo and Crane. When you're in that moment, you just look around and it's surreal. You really want to take a mental snapshot so you don't forget that."

Cubs Manager Joe Maddon

NL CHAMPIONSHIP SERIES

CUBS PRESIDENT THEO EPSTEIN (TOP, CENTER) AND MANAGER JOE MADDON MADE HISTORY IN CHICAGO BY GUIDING THE CUBS AND THEIR FANS TO THE FIRST PENNANT ON THE NORTH SIDE IN 70-PLUS YEARS. BRYANT (OPPOSITE) SINGLED IN A RUN IN THE CLINCHER.

WORLD SERIES

GAME 1, OCTOBER 25
CLEVELAND 6, CHICAGO 0

Entering the 2016 Fall Classic, it was guaranteed that a long-suffering fan base would finally lay claim to a World Series crown. The Cubs famously had not won a Fall Classic in 108 years, while the Indians' drought approached 68 seasons.

In Game 1, the underdog Tribe won with pitching yet again, as staff ace Corey Kluber tossed six scoreless innings in the club's 6-0 victory. "He's as good as they come," teammate Andrew Miller said.

The man they affectionately call "Klubot" punched out nine batters, including a World Series record eight in the first three innings. "It usually helps to win when Kluber's pitching, but we still have to win four games," said outfielder Rajai Davis. "We've got to go out there and pitch well, and play good defense."

Following the script set forth in the previous two rounds of the playoffs, Manager Terry Francona turned over the ball to relievers Miller and Cody Allen to finish the shutout with a convincing 15 combined K's.

The Cubs also had an ace on the mound in Jon Lester, but the Indians were able to get to the left-hander early with two runs in the first inning after a pair of walks, an RBI infield single from Jose Ramirez, and a hit-by-pitch from Brandon Guyer to cap the rally. Roberto Perez stretched the lead to 3-0 with a solo home run in the fourth, before blasting a three-run dinger in the eighth to put the game out of reach.

"[Perez] has gotten more aggressive lately and is swinging great," Davis said. "Going out there every day gives you confidence, and shows that your manager trusts you."

Francisco Lindor and Ramirez each collected three hits in the opening game. "I feel good when I'm not striking out," Ramirez said with a smile after the game. "I've always dreamed of being in the World Series, and that's what made this fun."

The win was Cleveland's first in a Fall Classic since Game 6 against the Marlins in 1997. The Cubs, meanwhile, had not won a World Series Game since Game 6 against Detroit in 1945, a string that would last at least one more game. Ben Zobrist boosted the visitors' offense with a double off Kluber in the second inning, one of his three hits on the night. Despite dominant Indians pitching, the Cubs put runners in scoring position five times — including two separate instances against Miller — but never could push a run across the plate.

"I liked our at-bats overall against Miller," Cubs Manager Joe Maddon said. "I liked that we got him up to nearly 50 pitches, also. There were a lot of positives with that. We struck out a lot, but I'll defend the fact that we had some good at-bats."

KYLE SCHWARBER (ABOVE) PLAYED IN HIS FIRST GAME SINCE APRIL AND DOUBLED OFF KLUBER (OPPOSITE, BOTTOM). CLEVELAND HOSTED ITS FIRST EVER WORLD SERIES GAME 1.

	1	2	3	4	5	6	7	8	9	R	H	E
CHICAGO	0	0	0	0	0	0	0	0	0	0	7	0
CLEVELAND	2	0	0	1	0	0	0	3	X	6	10	0

WP: Kluber **LP:** Lester
HR: CLE: Perez (2)

"[Kluber has] really mastered the art of the sinker-slider. And he's got a cutter in there, too, to keep you honest."

David Ross

AN ERA OF CHANGE

When two teams with upwards of 175 years of world title droughts combined meet in the World Series, there are bound to be a number of firsts. First Cubs World Series appearance in 71 years. First time the Tribe hosted Game 1 of a Fall Classic. But in 2016, it's unusual for first African-American player to play in the World Series for the Cubs to be on that list. Chicago leadoff man Dexter Fowler earned that distinction, though, when he stepped to the plate in Game 1 against the Indians' Corey Kluber.

"It's awesome," Fowler said. "Coming in and being the first African-American is always a staple piece."

His wife, Darya, shared her feelings on the significance of the event on Instagram. "On Tuesday, my husband should be standing at the plate, the first African-American Chicago Cub to bat in baseball's World Series," her post read. "My heart is full, and my throat holding back from crying with humble gratefulness."

The length of the aforementioned droughts, though, gives the situation context. In 1945, when the Cubs last played in the Fall Classic, Jackie Robinson was still two years away from breaking baseball's color barrier. And in 1948, the Indians squad that captured the title featured Larry Doby, the AL's first African-American player, and Satchel Paige, the first black man to pitch in the postseason. The duo became the first African-Americans in history to win a World Series.

Doby discussed the double-sided nature of such a distinction during his Cooperstown speech in 1998. "It's a very tough thing to look back and think about things that were probably negative. [But] you're proud and happy that you've been a part of integrating baseball to show people that we can live together, we can work together, we can play together and we can be successful together."

CUB FANS YOUNG AND OLD CAME OUT TO SUPPORT THEIR TEAM IN GAME 1, DESPITE THE FACT THAT THEY WERE PLAYING ON THE ROAD. LESTER (OPPOSITE) GOT THE START, BUT ALLOWED THREE EARNED RUNS TO THE INDIANS. LINDOR (ABOVE, SLIDING) WAS AN OFFENSIVE CATALYST FOR CLEVELAND, TALLYING THREE HITS.

"The first inning was tonight's game. Hopefully Jake picks me up tomorrow and gives me another chance at this."

Jon Lester

GAME 2, OCTOBER 26
CHICAGO 5, CLEVELAND 1

The Cubs took the adage "score early and often" to heart in Game 2, and less than 24 hours after being shut out in the Series opener, Chicago jumped out to an early lead at Progressive Field. Kris Bryant laced a single to center field in the top of the first, and his "Bryzzo" counterpart, Anthony Rizzo, battled through seven pitches before drilling a double to the right-field corner to drive him in all the way from first base.

"It's nice to score first, especially when you're the visiting team," Bryant said. "Take the momentum away; take the crowd out of it. To get up there and score within the first three batters is huge."

On a night when both clubs were bundled in base layers — the game time temperature registered at 43 degrees — the visitors proved that their bats had warmed up dramatically. By the time he was through with the second, Indians starter Trevor Bauer had already thrown more than 50 pitches, and the Cubs chased him after 3.2 innings of work — another short, albeit far less bloody, outing compared to his ALCS Game 3 showing.

Kyle Schwarber's bases-loaded RBI single in the top of the third increased his club's lead before the away boys broke the game open in the fifth. A night after he collected three hits, Ben Zobrist smacked a Zach McAllister offering into the right-field corner, and the ball caromed off the wall, allowing Rizzo — who had drawn a 10-pitch walk for his second free pass of the game — to score standing all the way from first. Schwarber then collected his second RBI single of the night,

knocking in Zobrist, before a wild pitch, a Jason Kipnis fielding error and a pair of walks conspired against Cleveland, allowing the Cubs to score their third run of the frame.

The Indians rotated through six relievers, with bullpen ace Andrew Miller unavailable after throwing more than 50 pitches in Game 1. "We saw a lot of their bullpen," said Bryant, "so we have a lot of information to use in the next game."

Francisco Lindor again proved to be a beacon of consistency for the Indians, reaching base on a free pass in the bottom of the first. And although his partner up the middle was uncharacteristically shaky in the field, committing an error and misplaying a potential double play, Kipnis scored Cleveland's only run. The second baseman cracked a double in the bottom of the sixth, advanced to third on a groundout, and scored on a wild pitch from Jake Arrieta. That proved to be Arrieta's only blemish, as he maintained a no-hitter through 5.1 innings to earn the victory in the Cubs' first World Series win since Game 6 in 1945. Neither club crossed the plate in the final three frames, and Aroldis Chapman entered in the eighth to close out the game.

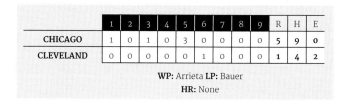

	1	2	3	4	5	6	7	8	9	R	H	E
CHICAGO	1	0	1	0	3	0	0	0	0	5	9	0
CLEVELAND	0	0	0	0	0	1	0	0	0	1	4	2

WP: Arrieta LP: Bauer
HR: None

"We knew [Schwarber] would contribute in some way, and that's why he's on the roster. Every at-bat he's had so far, he's worked the count, gotten a couple of walks and big hits. To just jump right into the World Series and have success, no big deal."

Kris Bryant

WORLD SERIES

SCHWARBER CONTINUED HIS TRIUMPHANT WORLD SERIES
RETURN IN GAME 2. THE SLUGGER REACHED BASE THREE
TIMES AND DROVE IN A PAIR OF RUNS.

RETURN OF THE LIVING DEAD

A pair of players who were all but left for dead — at least in terms of the post-season roster — showed in Game 2 why their respective managers believed in them in the first place.

After tearing his ACL and LCL in the season's third game, Cubs slugger Kyle Schwarber missed the remainder of the regular campaign and was left off the active roster for the first two rounds of the playoffs. Buzz about a potential return started, though, during the NLCS against the Dodgers, when he played in two Arizona Fall League games as a potential tune-up to see if he could be ready to join the Cubs in the World Series. On the day of Game 1, Manager Joe Maddon officially announced that Schwarber was indeed on the roster for the Fall Classic, and he went out that night and ripped a double off dominant Indians ace Corey Kluber.

Schwarber's return became even more dramatic in Game 2. He laced an RBI single off Indians starter Trevor Bauer in the third inning to give Chicago a 2-0 lead. Showing very little signs of rust despire not having faced live Major League pitching all season, Schwarber struck again in the fifth with an RBI single off Bryan Shaw, increasing the Cubs' lead to 4-0 to help put the game away.

"This is the moment we all lived for when we were little kids," Schwarber said. "We're here now, so we don't have anything to lose. I'm going to lay it on the line and see what happens."

The Indians also received a visit from the proverbial roster cemetery. Starting pitcher Danny Salazar, who missed most of September as well as the AL Division Series and ALCS with a forearm injury, saw his first World Series action with a scoreless inning of relief in the sixth.

"It takes a lot of pressure off when you see guys having quality at-bats. We did a good job tonight laying off some pitches and, when they made mistakes, hitting the ball hard."

Ben Zobrist

AFTER RIZZO (TOP RIGHT) OPENED THE SCORING WITH AN RBI DOUBLE IN THE FIRST, ZOBRIST (OPPOSITE), CONTINUED HIS HOT HITTING IN THE POSTSEASON, EXTENDING THE LEAD WITH AN RBI TRIPLE IN THE TOP OF THE FIFTH. THAT WAS MORE THAN ENOUGH RUN SUPPORT FOR THE CUBS' PITCHING STAFF, AS ARRIETA (BOTTOM) STRUCK OUT SIX AND HELD THE INDIANS TO ONE RUN BEFORE THE BULLPEN, LED BY CHAPMAN, SLAMMED THE DOOR.

GAME 3, OCTOBER 28
CLEVELAND 1, CHICAGO 0

Matters shifted to Wrigley Field for the first World Series game played there since 1945. Ready to unleash energy that had been building up for 71 years, the city of Chicago exploded in support of its North Siders, as tens of thousands of fans converged upon Wrigleyville several hours before game time.

With the Series tied, 1-1, and the next three games scheduled at the Friendly Confines, most experts picked the Cubs to take control. The underdog role, though, had been one the Indians were quite comfortable embracing, and they won an edge-of-their seats nail-biter, 1-0.

"I think we've been the underdog in every game and in every series," said reliever Bryan Shaw, who tossed 1.2 innings to help his team shut out the Cubs for the second time in the Series. "I feel like even when we were up, 3 games to none, over Toronto, people still expected them to come back. We feed off that. We enjoy it, and we play looser."

It was a game full of strategy and decisions from the outset. Cleveland Manager Terry Francona had the advantage of better opportunities, and he nailed each tough call perfectly, especially a pinch-hitting situation in the seventh inning.

Knotted in a scoreless tie and having the best arm of this postseason as the pitcher of record, Francona opted to pinch-hit for Andrew Miller with veteran Coco Crisp. With runners on first and third and just one out, Crisp came through with an RBI single to score the only run of the game.

As a brief reprieve from the shock of the first run crossing the plate for the visitors, actor and longtime Cubs devotee Bill Murray sang "Take Me Out to the Ball Game" during the seventh-inning stretch. The quirky Murray, who managed to work in Daffy Duck sound effects, was one of several celebrity baseball fans on hand, including Jon Hamm, Jesse Eisenberg and Eddie Vedder. But all they would witness at Wrigley was dominant Indians pitching.

Starter Josh Tomlin, Miller, Shaw and closer Cody Allen combined on the five-hitter. Ironically, the last 1-0 shutout in a World Series occurred in 2005, when Chicago's other team — the White Sox — beat the Astros by that score to complete their four-game sweep.

Francisco Lindor and Jose Ramirez each collected two hits for the Indians, but on a night when the wind was blowing firmly out of the park, it was the pitchers who ruled.

"Sometimes guys lick their chops a little too much during batting practice when they see the wind blowing out like that," said cleanup hitter Ben Zobrist, who stayed hot to record his sixth hit of his first 10 at-bats of this World Series. "But I don't think that was the case today. I think it was just really good pitching."

	1	2	3	4	5	6	7	8	9	R	H	E
CLEVELAND	0	0	0	0	0	0	1	0	0	1	8	1
CHICAGO	0	0	0	0	0	0	0	0	0	0	5	0

WP: Miller **LP:** Edwards Jr. **SV:** Allen
HR: None

"It was cool to see all the people outside Wrigley. And their energy stayed up all game."
Kyle Hendricks

WORLD SERIES

DECISIONS, DECISIONS

The choices made by managers Terry Francona and Joe Maddon had a major impact on the outcome of Game 3. Not only were there three manager replay challenges through the first six-and-a-half innings, but Francona also executed a pair of double-switches in his 10th career World Series victory.

It seemed as if the Cubs had the upper hand early on, when starter Kyle Hendricks caught Francisco Lindor taking a large lead off first base in the top of the first. Lindor was originally called safe, but Maddon asked the umpiring crew to review, and the call was overturned.

In the fifth, Francona pulled his first double-switch, summoning Andrew Miller from the 'pen while bringing Rajai Davis in to play left field for Carlos Santana. "The fact that I came in in the fifth is not a big deal," Miller said. "Tito puts the guys in good situations, and we trust that the plan is going to work out."

Cleveland's plan worked well in the top of the seventh, when Coco Crisp pinch-hit for Miller, who threw 1.1 innings, and knocked a single to right, scoring Michael Martinez. Martinez had nearly been picked off at third not long before — another call that Maddon challenged — but replay review upheld the original (safe) ruling. Immediately after Crisp's RBI, Jason Kipnis grounded to first, but the ball ricocheted off Anthony Rizzo and into the glove of Javier Baez, who was backing him up. Kipnis thought he beat Baez's throw to pitcher Mike Montgomery, and Francona agreed, but replay review upheld this call.

The eighth inning saw Maddon use Kyle Schwarber to pinch-hit and Francona juggle both his batting order and fielding configuration when Cody Allen came in to pitch, but it was the latter skipper who ultimately won this chess match to put the Series in the Indians' favor.

RELIEVER JUSTIN GRIMM (OPPOSITE, TOP) FACED JUST ONE BATTER IN THE FIFTH, BUT INDUCED AN INNING-ENDING DOUBLE PLAY IN WHICH ADDISON RUSSELL (ABOVE) FORCED OUT KIPNIS AT SECOND. ZOBRIST (OPPOSITE, BOTTOM) CONTRIBUTED IN LEFT FIELD WHILE ALSO COLLECTING ONE OF THE CUBS' FIVE HITS.

GAME 4, OCTOBER 29
CLEVELAND 7, CHICAGO 2

For the second night in a row, neither the situation nor the setting fazed the Indians, as ace Corey Kluber threw another six-inning gem to give his team a two-game edge in the Series. With the win, the Indians staff improved to 10-2 in the 2016 postseason with a paltry 1.68 ERA.

"I thought Kluber used his fastball even better today than the first game," said the Cubs' Kris Bryant. "I thought our bats would do better, but we gave [Indians pitchers] that ERA."

Chicago jumped out to an early lead after Dexter Fowler led off with a double, becoming the first player in history to hit three leadoff doubles in a single postseason. And although he came around to score on an Anthony Rizzo RBI single, the Cubs' bats largely went silent after that, scattering just five hits over the next eight frames.

Cleveland's dangerous lineup, on the other hand, gradually piled up runs against Cubs starter John Lackey. Carlos Santana popped a solo homer in the second to tie the game, and before the inning was over, the Indians had taken the lead. Lonnie Chisenhall reached base via a Bryant throwing error, took second on a fielder's choice, and scored when Kluber hit a dribbler down the third-base line, a play on which Bryant made another errant throw.

"He battled in that at-bat," said Jason Kipnis. "As a hitter, you're like, 'Kluber can't show us up, so we've got to step up.'"

One inning later, Kipnis did exactly that, smacking a double into the right-field corner. Francisco Lindor knocked him in with a single to center, his 16th hit of the postseason. The do-it-all short-stop then walked in the sixth and scored on a Chisenhall sac fly, giving Cleveland a three-run lead. During the regular season, the Indians were 70-1 in games during which they led by three or more runs.

That margin only increased in the top of the seventh, when Kipnis smashed a three-run homer to left on a

night when the wind was blowing in at Wrigley. "It was special," said Kipnis. "A Wrigley home run, a World Series home run — there are so many things I can check off on that one."

The Cubs showed some life in the bottom of the eighth when Fowler went yard to left-center, but it wouldn't be enough for the hometown team to pull out a victory against the Indians' lockdown bullpen.

"Fowler's at-bat was really good," said Andrew Miller, who allowed the blast but whiffed two to become the single-postseason leader in K's by a relief pitcher. "Obviously not ideal, but you move on. We have a lot of confidence in our guys."

	1	2	3	4	5	6	7	8	9	R	H	E
CLEVELAND	0	2	1	0	0	1	3	0	0	7	10	0
CHICAGO	1	0	0	0	0	0	0	1	0	2	7	2

WP: Kluber **LP:** Lackey

HR: CLE: Santana, Kipnis CHC: Fowler

FANS ON CHICAGO'S NORTH SIDE PACKED THE WRIGLEYVILLE NEIGHBOR-HOOD (OPPOSITE) PRIOR TO GAME 4 TO SEE IF THE CUBS COULD EVEN THE SERIES. FOWLER DID HIS PART IN THE CONTEST, KNOCKING A LEADOFF DOUBLE AND COMING AROUND TO SCORE BEFORE SMACKING A HOME RUN IN THE EIGHTH.

CELEBRITY CLASSIC

It's not just the average fans who waited their entire lifetime to see the Indians win the World Series or the Cubs just reach the World Series. Celebrity fans and athletes came out in droves for this historic match-up in which the participating teams were hoping to avoid a 68- (Indians) and 108-year (Cubs) title drought.

In Cleveland, the NBA champion Cavaliers, including LeBron James, showed up at Progressive Field to root on their home team a day after holding their ring ceremony. Actor John Cusack, famous for roles in movies like *Better Off Dead* and *Say Anything* and a lifelong Cubs fan, made the trek to Cleveland for Game 2. Actress Monica Potter, who most recently starred in the TV series "Parenthood," conversely, was born and bred in Cleveland and attended Game 2 while taking to Twitter to support the Tribe.

Once the Series moved to Wrigley, dozens of stars used their connections to experience the first Fall Classic games in Wrigley Field since 1945 firsthand: rockers Eddie Vedder, Billy Corgan and Tom Morello; comedians Jeff Garlin and Amy Schumer; and actors such as Bill Murray, Jon Hamm, Vince Vaughn, Gary Sinise, Jordana Brewster, Chris O'Donnell and Sophia Bush, to name just a few. They all came to witness history, but unfortunately for the majority of them rooting for the North Siders, the Indians spoiled the fans' World Series party in Games 3 and 4.

Thanks to the ballpark's seventh-inning stretch tradition, fans got to listen to Murray imitating Daffy Duck while singing "Take Me Out to the Ball Game" in Game 3, followed by Vaughn's rah-rah approach with the song in Game 4 and Vedder's showing off his famous pipes in Game 5. Just because the Tribe won the first two games at Wrigley, it didn't mean Chicagoans couldn't have some fun.

PLENTY OF FAMILIAR FACES WERE ON HAND TO SUPPORT THEIR CUBBIES IN GAME 4, INCLUDING CHICAGO BLACKHAWKS CAPTAIN JONATHAN TOEWS (TOP LEFT), ACTRESS BREWSTER (TOP RIGHT), MUSICIAN VEDDER (BOTTOM LEFT), HALL OF FAMER ANDRE DAWSON (BOTTOM RIGHT) AND COMEDIAN VAUGHN (CENTER). RIZZO (OPPOSITE) HIT AN RBI SINGLE IN THE FIRST.

"We know we've got to win out, but we've won three games in a row plenty of times. It can be done easily."

Kris Bryant

GAME 5, OCTOBER 30
CHICAGO 3, CLEVELAND 2

Seventy-one years was long enough. Finally, the Cubs gave their fans a World Series win at Wrigley Field for the first time since Game 6 in 1945. Facing elimination and a virtually invincible Cleveland bullpen, Chicago tagged starter Trevor Bauer for three runs in the fourth, and Aroldis Chapman hurled an eight-out save to help the Cubs hold on for the 3-2 win.

"We wanted to acknowledge the fans," Anthony Rizzo said of the impromptu curtain call the team gave the crowd after the game, which was the last to take place in the Friendly Confines this season. "They brought the noise tonight. There was a lot of nervous energy."

Like many of Cleveland's 2016 postseason affairs, the Game 5 matchup looked on paper like a mismatch in favor of

PEARL JAM'S EDDIE VEDDER (ABOVE), AN ILLINOIS NATIVE, BROUGHT WRIGLEY TO ITS FEET DURING THE SEVENTH-INNING STRETCH. LESTER (OPPOSITE) EARNED THE W.

the Cubs. Veteran Jon Lester entered the contest 8-7 with a 2.60 ERA in 20 career postseason starts. Bauer toed the rubber for the Indians with a 0-1 career record and 5.00 ERA in three prior October outings.

Never deterred by long odds, the Indians showed early how they had given themselves a 3-games-to-1 Series advantage through four games. Unsung hero and third baseman Jose Ramirez struck again, launching a two-out solo home run in the second inning after Lester had overpowered the game's first five hitters. The blast silenced the boisterous Wrigley crowd, and more importantly staked Bauer to a 1-0 lead. Cleveland entered this game 8-0 in the postseason when scoring first, and with Ramirez's homer, the Indians also became the first team in postseason history to have four switch-hitters go deep.

The Cubs got to Bauer in the fourth, though, sparked by a leadoff homer from Kris Bryant, who had been relatively quiet in the World Series up to that point. A Rizzo double, three singles — two of them of the infield variety — and a sac fly later, and the Cubs had grabbed a 3-1 lead, finally giving the Wrigley faithful hope that they could extend the Series.

"[Bauer] was cruising through the first three innings," Bryant said. "So it was nice to have a big inning there, get us going a little bit."

The Indians, of course, bounced right back, stringing together two singles and a stolen base to rattle Lester and cross the plate once in the sixth, tightening the score to 3-2.

From there, both teams' closers took over early. Managers Joe Maddon and Terry Francona brought in Aroldis Chapman and Cody Allen, respectively, with just one out in the seventh, but it was Chapman who inherited a lead that he would preserve through the final eight outs.

	1	2	3	4	5	6	7	8	9	R	H	E
CLEVELAND	0	1	0	0	0	1	0	0	0	2	6	1
CHICAGO	0	0	0	3	0	0	0	0	X	3	7	0

WP: Lester **LP:** Bauer **SV:** Chapman
HR: CLE: Ramirez CHC: Bryant

"I'm excited that Jon Lester pitched the way he did. It was really as good of a game as he's pitched all year. He brought it to them."

David Ross

THE BIG INNING

Three proved to be the magic number for both the Cubs and the Indians in four of the Series' first five games, as the winning team enjoyed a single inning during which it scored three times in every contest except Game 3.

Cleveland won the World Series opener definitively, thanks to an eighth-inning, three-run homer by backstop Roberto Perez — his second longball of the game — to put the Indians ahead, 6-0. Then came Game 2, when Chicago chipped away at a pair of Indians pitchers in the top of the fifth. Ben Zobrist added to his club's two-run lead with an RBI triple before Kyle Schwarber knocked him in with a single to center. Reliever Bryan Shaw then walked Addison Russell with the bases loaded for the third run of the frame, giving the away boys a 5-0 edge in a game that they ultimately won, 5-1.

"We had a lot of base runners on, and we could have scored a lot more," said Zobrist.

After escaping with a 1-0 victory when the Series flipped from Progressive Field to Wrigley, the Indians took a 3-games-to-1 advantage in Game 4 thanks to a three-run, seventh-inning Jason Kipnis blast.

But the Cubs triumphed in their final opportunity at home when their bats came alive in the fourth inning. Kris Bryant, Anthony Rizzo, Zobrist and Russell reached base in succession, and retiring catcher David Ross contributed a sacrifice fly to provide all the runs their team would need to play at least one more game.

"We gave up three runs and had a chance to win the ballgame a couple different times," said Indians starting pitcher Trevor Bauer. "We didn't come through tonight."

AFTER BRYANT (OPPOSITE, TOP) SMASHED A SOLO HOMER IN THE CUBS' THREE-RUN FOURTH, CHAPMAN (ABOVE) CAME ON IN RELIEF. THE FLAME THROWER FIRED 2.2 INNINGS OF SHUTOUT BALL TO NOTCH THE SAVE AND SECURE A WIN FOR THE HOMETOWN CROWD.

"I felt like our at-bats after the fourth inning were just as good. So that's a good sign for us."

Kris Bryant

GAME 6, NOVEMBER 1
CHICAGO 9, CLEVELAND 3

If the pitching matchup for Game 6 back at Progressive Field seemed lopsided in the Cubs' favor, that's because it was. On the heels of a 3-2, Game 5 victory, Chicago hopped all over Indians starter Josh Tomlin — who was pitching on three days' rest for the first time in his career — for a three-run first inning, punctuated by a Kris Bryant solo shot to left-field, which according to Statcast traveled 433 feet. Ace Jake Arrieta, on the other hand, held Cleveland hitless for the first three frames, less than a week after tossing 5.1 innings of no-hit ball in Game 2.

Bryant's blast began a two-out rally in which Anthony Rizzo and Ben Zobrist smacked back-to-back singles and came around to score on an Addison Russell two-run double. The ball looked like it could have been caught, but center fielder Tyler Naquin and right fielder Lonnie Chisenhall had a bit of a mis-communication and it dropped in between them, adding to the Cubs' early lead.

Two innings later, Chicago virtually assured that there would be a Game 7, loading the bases on a Kyle Schwarber walk and another pair of singles from Rizzo and Zobrist. That set the stage for Russell, who delivered a mammoth grand slam to center that traveled a foot further than Bryant's ball, giving the visitors a seven-run lead.

"That was the hit of the night there," said Bryant. "Any time you get four runs on one swing, [that's] huge. He's had a lot of big home runs this postseason. He's kind of been the catalyst for us."

Russell became the first player to hit a Fall Classic grand slam since Paul Konerko did so for the White Sox in 2005, and the longball gave him six RBI on the night, tying the record for a single Series game.

"We've been doing this all year, been breaking records, been putting new history in history books," said Russell.

Jason Kipnis put the home team on the board in the fourth when he broke up Arrieta's no-hit bid with a double and scored on a Mike Napoli single. And the second baseman also took responsibility for the Indians' second run of the game when he popped a solo homer the very next frame.

But when the ninth inning rolled around, Chicago's corner infielders demanded that the Series go the distance. With two outs, Bryant singled to finish his night 4 for 5 at the plate, and Rizzo promptly launched a two-run homer to right to cap the Cubs' victory.

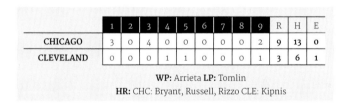

	1	2	3	4	5	6	7	8	9	R	H	E
CHICAGO	3	0	4	0	0	0	0	0	2	9	13	0
CLEVELAND	0	0	0	1	1	0	0	0	1	3	6	1

WP: Arrieta **LP:** Tomlin
HR: CHC: Bryant, Russell, Rizzo CLE: Kipnis

"Throughout the whole year, being part of the Cubs, you're put in the limelight. And early on, you're forced to deliver whenever the game's on the line. I think tomorrow we're going to come to the clubhouse with a lot of confidence and a lot of energy. Game 7, it's a kid's dream."

Addison Russell

WORLD SERIES

MR. NOVEMBER

It was 74 degrees in Cleveland for the start of Game 6 — hardly bone-chilling — but the calendar read November 1, nonetheless. With Reggie Jackson already owning the moniker of "Mr. October," several players in history, including three this year, have made their case to be named "Mr. November."

In Game 6, the Cubs' Addison Russell and Kris Bryant (opposite), along with the Indians' Jason Kipnis, campaigned for the title. Russell tied a World Series single-game record with six RBI, which came via a misplayed fly ball that was ruled a two-run double and a grand slam that gave Chicago a 7-0 lead. Bryant led the scoring barrage with a solo home run in the first and went 4 for 5 on the night.

And while the Tribe took a beating, 9-3, Kipnis certainly did all he could, going 3 for 5 with a double, homer and two runs scored. The trio's efforts fit in among MLB's top November performances:

1. Addison Russell; Nov. 1, 2016; Game 6
Grand slam, 6 RBI

2. Derek Jeter; Oct. 31*, 2001; Game 4
Game-winning HR
*12:04 a.m. on Nov. 1

3. Luis Gonzalez; Nov. 4, 2001; Game 7
Game-winning RBI single

4. Hideki Matsui; Nov. 4, 2009; Game 6
3 for 4, 6 RBI

5. Tim Lincecum; Nov. 1, 2010; Game 5
8 IP, 1 R, 10 K's

6. Scott Brosius; Nov. 1, 2001; Game 5
Game-tying HR

7. Randy Johnson; Nov. 3, 2001; Game 6
7 IP, 2 R, 7 K's

8. Chase Utley; Nov. 2, 2009; Game 5
2 HR, 4 RBI

9. Eric Hosmer; Nov. 1, 2015; Game 5
Mad dash home

10. Johnny Damon; Nov. 1, 2009; Game 4
3 H, 2 R, 2 SB

ARRIETA (TOP) RECEIVED PLENTY OF RUN SUPPORT WHILE SUPPRESSING THE INDIANS' OFFENSE, FIRING 5.2 INNINGS OF TWO-RUN BALL TO NOTCH HIS SECOND WIN OF THE WORLD SERIES. RIZZO KNOCKED THREE HITS, INCLUDING A HOME RUN IN THE NINTH INNING, AND SCORED THREE TIMES AS THE CUBS EVENED THE SERIES AT THREE GAMES APIECE.

WORLD SERIES

"When we were down, 3-1, it was take it a game at a time and try to get to Game 7. Tomorrow we're going to be there, and it's nice to build off these last two games with momentum."

Kris Bryant

GAME 7, NOVEMBER 2
CHICAGO 8, CLEVELAND 7, 10 INNINGS

The excitement and, frankly, anxiety, surrounding Game 7 could be felt hours before game time. The Indians had not won a World Series since 1948 and the Cubs' dry spell dated back to 1908, so fans could easily be forgiven if they were a little more nervous than fired up.

After the Indians — who came from behind to win 38 times during the season — battled back from a 5-1 deficit to tie the game, the Cubs' bats prevailed, plating two runs in the 10th on an RBI double by eventual Series MVP Ben Zobrist and an RBI single by Miguel Montero.

The Tribe, of course, fought back with a run in the bottom of the 10th, but a pair of relievers shut the door and brought the Cubs their first world title in 108 years.

"We've been listening to the Rocky soundtrack the last two games," said Zobrist. "We have our own Italian Stallion in Anthony Rizzo, who's been putting the music on. It was a heavyweight fight. The Indians matched us blow for blow."

Once the game began — just the 10th in MLB history to start in November — Dexter Fowler fired the first shot, a lead-off home run in the first inning off Indians ace Corey Kluber. The bomb was the first ever to open a Game 7. It emboldened the enormous amount of Cubs fans at Cleveland's Progressive Field to make their presence heard. A "Let's Go Cubs" chant reached such a decibel level that it sounded like Chicago was the home team, but was quickly countered with a thunderous "Let's Go Tribe."

Carlos Santana laced an RBI single off NL ERA champ Kyle Hendricks to tie the game in the third, but the Cubs struck repeatedly with two runs in both the fourth and fifth innings.

Starting his third game of the Series, Kluber just didn't have the gas or sharpness he had shown in Games 1 and 4. Javier Baez blasted a homer to center field to lead off the fifth, and the Indians' ace was lifted in favor of Andrew Miller.

Miller didn't fare much better against the Cubs' suddenly hot bats, and an RBI single from Anthony Rizzo gave them a 5-1 lead.

With Jon Lester and Aroldis Chapman pitching in relief, Cleveland rallied for two in the fifth and three in the eighth, highlighted by a Rajai Davis two-run, game-tying home run

just over the left-field wall, as each team's stoppers took their lumps.

"The Cubs beat up on Miller tonight, and got to their other guys because the Cubs are good," Maddon said. "The Indians got to Chapman because the Indians are good."

Rain slowed down the momentum for about 17 minutes after the ninth, but the Cubs rallied against Bryan Shaw in the 10th to put themselves in position to close it out, sending fans in Wrigleyville into hysteria.

	1	2	3	4	5	6	7	8	9	10	R	H	E
CHICAGO	1	0	0	2	2	1	0	0	0	2	8	13	3
CLEVELAND	0	0	1	0	2	0	0	3	0	1	7	11	1

WP: Chapman **LP:** Shaw **SV:** Montgomery
HR: CHC: Fowler, Baez, Ross CLE: Davis

CUBS FANS AT PROGRESSIVE FIELD CELEBRATED THE VICTORY THAT MARKED THE END OF A 108-YEAR WORLD SERIES DROUGHT.

"So many generations have gone through this. So many people in Chicago are thinking of their fathers and grandfathers. It's bigger than these 25 guys. It's about the organization."

Cubs General Manager Jed Hoyer

(CLOCKWISE FROM TOP LEFT) FOWLER WAS FIRED UP AS HE ROUNDED THE BASES ON HIS SOLO HOME RUN IN THE FIRST INNING TO PUT THE CUBS ON THE BOARD. HENDRICKS FIRED 63 PITCHES IN 4.2 INNINGS TO FINISH THE POSTSEASON WITH A 1.42 ERA. BRYANT SLID UNDER THE INDIANS' ROBERTO PEREZ'S TAG TO SCORE ON RUSSELL'S SAC FLY IN THE FOURTH INNING.

ZOBI, MVP

Up and down the Cubs' roster, player after player was worthy of MVP consideration. But as the champagne bottles popped and chants of "Go Cubs Go" resonated throughout Progressive Field, it was Ben Zobrist who unassumingly stepped into the spotlight to claim his World Series MVP Award, which was partially voted on by fans for the first time in MLB history.

The 35-year-old utility man, who won his second straight title after being a valuable member of the 2015 world champion Royals, truly proved that he could do it all this season, playing six different positions across the diamond. During the World Series, he started every game in left field, but it was at the plate where his contributions resonated most.

Heading into Game 7, Zobrist owned a .391 average and .462 OBP over 23 World Series at-bats. He boasted nine hits, most notably an RBI triple in Game 2, to help Chicago secure its first win on the road. But with the Series on the line, Zobrist stepped up in a big way, smacking a 10th-inning RBI double down the left-field line to score Albert Almora Jr., who was pinch-running for Kyle Schwarber.

"The guy was hitting .400 in the World Series," said Almora. "[He's] an unbelievable hitter and an unbelievable player in general. When I was on second and he was hitting, I knew once he hit it that I was going to score."

The hit was Zobrist's only knock in five at-bats on the night, but it brought his slugging percentage for the Series to .500, tying him with Kris Bryant for the second-best mark on the team, behind Rizzo (.600), and making him the first-ever Cubs player to take home World Series MVP honors.

"This one about made me pass out. I feel like the way the Series was up and down, then getting up early in Game 7, then it getting away in the eighth, then scoring two in the 10th, it was an epic battle."

Ben Zobrist

PROGRESSIVE FIELD WAS FILLED WITH CELEBRITY CUBS FANS SUCH AS EDDIE VEDDER AND BILL MURRAY (TOP LEFT). BAEZ (TOP RIGHT) CRACKED A HOME RUN IN THE FIFTH. WORLD SERIES MVP ZOBRIST (BOTTOM) DELIVERED A CLUTCH RBI DOUBLE IN THE 10TH.

DAVID ROSS (TOP LEFT) ROUNDED THE BASES AFTER HITTING A SOLO HOME RUN IN THE SIXTH INNING. RIZZO (TOP RIGHT) CELEBRATED AFTER HITTING AN RBI SINGLE IN THE FIFTH. MONTERO (BOTTOM) HIT AN RBI SINGLE IN THE 10TH.

WORLD SERIES

ZOBRIST WAS AWARDED
WORLD SERIES MVP
AFTER HITTING .357
WITH A .919 OPS IN THE
SEVEN GAME SET
AGAINST THE INDIANS.

"It has nothing to do with curses or superstitions. It has everything to do with right now."

Cubs Manager Joe Maddon

POSTSEASON STATS

NO.	PLAYER	W	L	ERA	WHIP	SO	SV
	PITCHERS						
49	JAKE ARRIETA	2	1	3.63	1.07	25	0
54	AROLDIS CHAPMAN	2	0	3.45	1.09	21	4
6	CARL EDWARDS JR.	0	1	2.84	1.42	4	0
52	JUSTIN GRIMM	0	0	12.46	1.62	3	0
28	KYLE HENDRICKS	1	1	1.42	1.03	19	0
41	JOHN LACKEY	0	1	4.85	1.54	12	0
34	JON LESTER	3	1	2.02	0.93	30	0
38	MIKE MONTGOMERY	1	1	3.14	1.47	11	1
56	HECTOR RONDON	1	0	4.50	1.50	5	0
46	PEDRO STROP	0	0	3.18	1.06	3	0
37	TRAVIS WOOD	1	0	2.84	1.11	7	0

NO.	PLAYER	AB	H	AVG	HR	RBI	OBP
	CATCHERS						
40	WILLSON CONTRERAS	39	10	.256	1	5	.326
47	MIGUEL MONTERO	12	2	.167	1	5	.167
3	DAVID ROSS	16	4	.250	2	4	.300
	INFIELDERS						
9	JAVIER BAEZ	68	18	.265	2	8	.282
17	KRIS BRYANT	65	20	.308	3	8	.400
2	TOMMY LA STELLA	1	0	.000	0	0	.000
44	ANTHONY RIZZO	65	18	.277	3	10	.373
27	ADDISON RUSSELL	64	13	.203	3	13	.235
	OUTFIELDERS						
5	ALBERT ALMORA JR.	10	0	.000	0	0	.000
8	CHRIS COGHLAN	7	0	.000	0	0	.125
24	DEXTER FOWLER	72	18	.250	3	6	.280
22	JASON HEYWARD	48	5	.104	0	1	.140
12	KYLE SCHWARBER	17	7	.412	0	2	.500
68	JORGE SOLER	13	2	.154	0	0	.313
18	BEN ZOBRIST	64	16	.250	0	5	.319

BIRTH OF THE CUBS

In 1914, the independent, six-team Federal League began play as a Major League in six cities, including Chicago. The Chicago Federals, or Chi-Feds, enjoyed just a brief tenure, but ultimately helped lead to the development of the Cubs franchise we know today. After all, the Chi-Feds paid $1.92 million to acquire "[a] ninety-nine year lease on the property ... very advantageously located for a baseball park" at Clark and Addison. And although the team vanished after its second MLB season, its former owner, Charles Weeghman, assembled a group of investors to buy the Cubs. Among them: William Wrigley Jr.

Under former owner Charles W. Murphy, the Cubs had been successful on the field. They captured the NL pennant in 1906, winning 116 games — a record now shared with the 2001 Seattle Mariners — but shockingly lost the World Series (the first ever Crosstown Classic) to an underdog White Sox team known as the "Hitless Wonders." They recovered to win the world championship in 1907 and again in '08, and the first of seven additional modern-era pennants in 1910.

On April 20, 1916, the Joe Tinker–led Cubs moved into the ballpark now known as Wrigley Field and won the first National League game there, defeating the Reds, 7-6, in 11 innings. Wrigley then hosted World Series trips every three years for nearly two decades — in 1929, '32, '35 and '38 — and again in 1945, but there were no Cubs victories to be had. Future Hall of Famers like Ernie Banks, Ron Santo, Fergie Jenkins, Billy Williams and Ryne Sandberg came and went without a ring, before Chicago's North Side franchise made its intentions to end the Curse of the Billy Goat. The 2015 club reached the NLCS on the strength of a dynamic young squad, but ultimately it was the 2016 group that sealed the deal to vanquish the Cubs' 108-year title drought once and for all.

FROM LEFT: HARRY STEINFELDT JOINED THE FAMOUS DOUBLE PLAY TRIO OF SHORTSTOP TINKER, SECOND BASEMAN JOHNNY EVERS AND FIRST BASEMAN FRANK CHANCE IN THE CUBS' INFIELD FROM 1906–10.

CHICAGO CUBS POSTSEASON HISTORY

BROWN WAS THE CUBS' ACE DURING THEIR TITLE RUNS IN THE EARLY 1900s. THE HALL OF FAMER POSTED AN ERA BELOW 2.00 SIX TIMES IN HIS CAREER AND LED THE LEAGUE WITH A 1.04 MARK IN 1906.

1906

WORLD SERIES
CHICAGO WHITE SOX 4, CUBS 2

October 9 White Sox 2 at Cubs 1
October 10 Cubs 7 at White Sox 1
October 11 White Sox 3 at Cubs 0
October 12 Cubs 1 at White Sox 0
October 13 White Sox 8 at Cubs 6
October 14 Cubs 3 at White Sox 8

1907

WORLD SERIES
CUBS 4, DETROIT TIGERS 0

October 8 Tigers 3 at Cubs 3
October 9 Tigers 1 at Cubs 3
October 10 Tigers 1 at Cubs 5
October 11 Cubs 6 at Tigers 1
October 12 Cubs 2 at Tigers 0

Entering the 1907 season, the Cubs were still searching for their first world title, fresh off a Fall Classic defeat at the hands of the crosstown rival White Sox, who were known as the "Hitless Wonders." Sporting nearly the same roster as they did in 1906 when they won 116 games, the Frank Chance-managed North Siders finished the regular-season with 107 victories to take the National League pennant by an astounding 17-game margin.

The World Series between the Tigers and Cubs opened at Chicago's West Side Grounds, and Game 1 finished in unique fashion: a 3-3 tie. But from there on out, the Cubs took control, winning four straight games by a combined score of 16-3 to claim the franchise's first title.

Chicago pitchers Mordecai Brown, Orval Overall, Jack Pfiester and Ed Reulbach claimed victories, while infielder Harry Steinfeldt would have easily claimed the Series MVP Award had it existed at the time, as he batted .471 with a 1.197 OPS.

1908

WORLD SERIES
CUBS 4, DETROIT TIGERS 1
October 10 Cubs 10 at Tigers 6
October 11 Tigers 1 at Cubs 6
October 12 Tigers 8 at Cubs 3

October 13 Cubs 3 at Tigers 0
October 14 Cubs 2 at Tigers 0

The year 1908 marked just the fifth time the World Series was officially played and served as the third consecutive postseason in which the Chicago Cubs were competing. During the World Series, the Cubs sought to become the first team in Major League history to win back-to-back world championships. In a rematch of the 1097 Fall Classic, they again faced the Tigers, who were out to avenge the previous season's loss and march away with a title.

In all, the Cubs would come out on top, winning the Series, 4 games to 1. With the title, the Cubs established themselves as the first modern dynasty in baseball. Chicago second baseman Johnny Evers proved to be an offensive sparkplug, posting the third-highest batting average (.350) on the team during the five-game set. The then-27-year-old — who enjoyed the second-best season of his career that year in terms of batting average (.300) and OPS (.777) — recorded an impressive seven hits and two RBI in the Fall Classic, and scored five times.

THE 1906 CUBS TEAM IS STILL REGARDED AS ONE OF THE BEST, IF NOT THE BEST, IN BASEBALL HISTORY. THE CLUB'S 116 WINS ARE STILL TIED FOR THE MOST ALL TIME, MATCHED ONLY BY THE SEATTLE MARINERS IN 2001.

FIRST BASEMAN FRED MERKLE WAS A MEMBER OF THE CUBS TEAM THAT MADE THE WORLD SERIES IN 1918. CHICAGO LOST IN SIX GAMES, BUT NEITHER TEAM SCORED MORE THAN THREE RUNS IN ANY CONTEST, AND THE RED SOX SCORED ONLY NINE IN TOTAL, THE FEWEST BY A WINNING TEAM IN WORLD SERIES HISTORY.

On the mound, Mordecai Brown and Orval Overall, also standouts in the 1907 Series, claimed two wins apiece and recorded back-to-back shutouts in Games 4 and 5 to secure the title.

1910

WORLD SERIES
PHILADELPHIA ATHLETICS 4, CUBS 1
October 17 Cubs 1 at Athletics 4
October 18 Cubs 3 at Athletics 9
October 20 Athletics 12 at Cubs 5
October 22 Athletics 3 at Cubs 4
October 23 Athletics 7 at Cubs 2

1918

WORLD SERIES
BOSTON RED SOX 4, CUBS 2
September 5 Red Sox 1 at Cubs 0
September 6 Red Sox 1 at Cubs 3
September 7 Red Sox 2 at Cubs 1
September 9 Cubs 2 at Red Sox 3
September 10 Cubs 3 at Red Sox 0
September 11 Cubs 1 at Red Sox 2

1929

WORLD SERIES
PHILADELPHIA ATHLETICS 4, CUBS 1
October 8 Athletics 3 at Cubs 1
October 9 Athletics 9 at Cubs 3
October 11 Cubs 3 at Athletics 1
October 12 Cubs 8 at Athletics 10
October 14 Cubs 2 at Athletics 3

1932

WORLD SERIES

POSTSEASON HISTORY

NEW YORK YANKEES 4, CUBS 0
- **September 28** Cubs 6 at Yankees 12
- **September 29** Cubs 2 at Yankees 5
- **October 1** Yankees 7 at Cubs 5
- **October 2** Yankees 13 at Cubs 6

1935

WORLD SERIES
DETROIT TIGERS 4, CUBS 2
- **October 2** Cubs 3 at Tigers 0
- **October 3** Cubs 3 at Tigers 8
- **October 4** Tigers 6 at Cubs 5
- **October 5** Tigers 2 at Cubs 1
- **October 6** Tigers 1 at Cubs 3
- **October 7** Cubs 3 at Tigers 4

1938

WORLD SERIES
NEW YORK YANKEES 4, CUBS 0
- **October 5** Yankees 3 at Cubs 1
- **October 6** Yankees 6 at Cubs 3
- **October 8** Cubs 2 at Yankees 5
- **October 9** Cubs 3 at Yankees 8

1945

WORLD SERIES
DETROIT TIGERS 4, CUBS 3
- **October 3** Cubs 9 at Tigers 0
- **October 4** Cubs 1 at Tigers 4
- **October 5** Cubs 3 at Tigers 0
- **October 6** Tigers 4 at Cubs 1
- **October 7** Tigers 8 at Cubs 4
- **October 8** Tigers 7 at Cubs 8
- **October 10** Tigers 9 at Cubs 3

THE CUBS FOUGHT HARD AGAINST THE PHILADELPHIA ATHLETICS IN THE 1929 WORLD SERIES BUT ULTIMATELY CAME UP SHORT. THE HOME TEAM PLATED THREE RUNS IN THE NINTH, PUNCTUATED BY BING MILLER'S WALK-OFF DOUBLE, TO WIN A TIGHT 3-2 CONTEST AND TAKE THE TITLE AT SHIBE PARK.

CLOSER HECTOR RONDON AND BATTERY MATE MIGUEL MONTERO EMBRACED IN CELEBRATION OF THE CUBS' CLINCHING AN NLCS BERTH IN 2015. THE ACHIEVEMENT MARKED THE FIRST TIME THE CLUB ADVANCED TO THE LEAGUE CHAMPIONSHIP SERIES IN MORE THAN A DECADE.

POSTSEASON HISTORY

1984

NLCS

SAN DIEGO PADRES 3, CUBS 2

    October 2 Padres 0 at Cubs 13

    October 3 Padres 2 at Cubs 4

    October 4 Cubs 1 at Padres 7

    October 6 Cubs 5 at Padres 7

    October 7 Cubs 3 at Padres 6

1989

NLCS

SAN FRANCISCO GIANTS 4, CUBS 1

    October 4 Giants 11 at Cubs 3

    October 5 Giants 5 at Cubs 9

    October 7 Cubs 4 at Giants 5

    October 8 Cubs 4 at Giants 6

    October 9 Cubs 2 at Giants 3

1998

NLDS

ATLANTA BRAVES 3, CUBS 0

    September 30 Cubs 1 at Braves 7

    October 1 Cubs 1 at Braves 2

    October 3 Braves 6 at Cubs 2

2003

NLDS

CUBS 3, BRAVES 2

    September 30 Cubs 4 at Braves 2

    October 1 Cubs 3 at Braves 5

    October 3 Braves 1 at Cubs 3

    October 4 Braves 6 at Cubs 4

    October 5 Braves 1 at Cubs 5

NLCS

FLORIDA MARLINS 4, CUBS 3

    October 7 Marlins 9 at Cubs 8

    October 8 Marlins 3 at Cubs 12

    October 10 Cubs 5 at Marlins 4

    October 11 Cubs 8 at Marlins 3

    October 12 Cubs 0 at Marlins 4

    October 14 Marlins 8 at Cubs 3

    October 15 Marlins 9 at Cubs 6

2007

NLDS

ARIZONA DIAMONDBACKS 3, CUBS 0

    October 3 Cubs 1 at D-backs 3

    October 4 Cubs 4 at D-backs 8

    October 6 D-backs 5 at Cubs 1

2008

NLDS

LOS ANGELES DODGERS 3, CUBS 0

    October 1 Dodgers 7 at Cubs 2

    October 2 Dodgers 10 at Cubs 3

    October 4 Cubs 1 at Dodgers 3

2015

WILD CARD

CUBS VS. PITTSBURGH PIRATES

    October 7 Cubs 4 at Pirates 0

NLDS

CUBS 3, ST. LOUIS CARDINALS 1

    October 9 Cubs 0 at Cardinals 4

    October 10 Cubs 6 at Cardinals 3

    October 12 Cardinals 6 at Cubs 8

    October 13 Cardinals 4 at Cubs 6

NLCS

NEW YORK METS 4, CUBS 0

    October 17 Cubs 2 at Mets 4

    October 18 Cubs 1 at Mets 4

    October 20 Mets 5 at Cubs 2

    October 21 Mets 8 at Cubs 3

HOW THE CUBS WERE BUILT

The Cubs' championship roster was carefully stitched together with high draft picks, key free-agent signings and intricate trades. Chicago likely wouldn't have won the World Series without its potent pitching staff, which was assembled thanks to some prescient deals. Jake Arrieta, the 2015 NL Cy Young winner, was acquired from the Orioles three years ago, while Kyle Hendricks arrived via Texas in 2012. Jason Hammel, John Lackey and Jon Lester signed as free agents in the last two offseasons alone. The finishing touches on the mound involved bullpen additions, highlighted by the acquisition of Aroldis Chapman a week before the 2016 trade deadline.

General Manager Theo Epstein and the front office built the infield on the bedrock of some impressive scouting. Catcher Willson Contreras signed as an amateur free agent out of Venezuela; Javier Baez and Kris Bryant were both first-round draft picks; Anthony Rizzo was acquired via trade before signing a big contract in 2013; and Addison Russell came to Chicago in 2014 in a trade with the Oakland A's. In the outfield, Chicago benefited greatly from free-agent pickups, with the exception of Albert Almora Jr., another first round selection.

Finally, to shore up their lineup, the Cubs added veterans — David Ross, Miguel Montero and Ben Zobrist, among others — to bring experience and firepower to Wrigley Field. This blend of players came together in magical fashion to bring the North Side of Chicago their first title in 108 years.

DRAFT

ALBERT ALMORA JR.	1st round, 2012
JAVIER BAEZ	1st round, 2011
KRIS BRYANT	1st round, 2013
KYLE SCHWARBER	1st round, 2014
MATT SZCZUR	5th round, 2010
ROB ZASTRYZNY	2nd round, 2013

FREE AGENCY

TREVOR CAHILL	1 year/$4.25M (2016)
WILLSON CONTRERAS	As an amateur free agent (2009)
DEXTER FOWLER	1 year/$13M (2016)
JASON HAMMEL	2 years/$20M (2015)
JASON HEYWARD	8 years/$184M (2016)
MUNENORI KAWASAKI	Minor League contract (2016)
JOHN LACKEY	2 years/$32M (2016)
JON LESTER	6 years/$155M (2015)
DAVID ROSS	2 years/$5M (2015)
JORGE SOLER	9 years/$30M (2012)
BEN ZOBRIST	4 years/$56M (2016)

RULE 5 DRAFT

HECTOR RONDON	From CLE, 2012

TRADES

JAKE ARRIETA	From BAL with Pedro Strop and cash for Steve Clevenger and Scott Feldman (2013)
AROLDIS CHAPMAN	From NYY for Rashad Crawford, Billy McKinney, Gleyber Torres and Adam Warren (2016)
CHRIS COGHLAN	From OAK for Arismendy Alcantara (2016)
CARL EDWARDS JR.	From TEX with Justin Grimm, Mike Olt and Neil Ramirez for Matt Garza (2013)
JUSTIN GRIMM	From TEX with Carl Edwards Jr., Mike Olt and Neil Ramirez for Matt Garza (2013)
KYLE HENDRICKS	From TEX with Christian Villanueva for Ryan Dempster (2012)
TOMMY LA STELLA	From ATL for Arodys Vizcaino (2014)
MIGUEL MONTERO	From ARI for Jeferson Mejia and Zack Godley (2014)
MIKE MONTGOMERY	From SEA with Jordan Pries for Paul Blackburn and Dan Vogelbach (2016)
SPENCER PATTON	From TEX for Frandy De La Rosa (2015)
ANTHONY RIZZO	From San Diego with Zach Cates for Andrew Cashner and Kyung-Min Na (2012)
ADDISON RUSSELL	From OAK with Billy McKinney, Dan Straily and cash for Jason Hammel and Jeff Samardzija (2014)
JOE SMITH	From LAA for Jesus Castillo (2016)
PEDRO STROP	From BAL with Jake Arrieta and cash for Steve Clevenger and Scott Feldman (2013)
TRAVIS WOOD	From CIN with Dave Sappelt and Ronald Torreyes for Sean Marshall (2011)

JOE MADDON

MANAGER

The 2015 NL Manager of the Year, Maddon is known around the league for his unconventional approach to the game. But his tactics get results, as the club has won 200 regular-season games in just the past two seasons under his tutelage.

70

ALBERT ALMORA JR.

OUTFIELD

The No. 6 overall pick in the 2012 Draft, Almora debuted in early June and hit three home runs while shoring up Chicago's outfield defense.

5

JAKE ARRIETA

PITCHER

Arrieta authored his second career no-hitter in April and dominated from then on, as his marks in ERA and WHIP ranked among the National League's top 10. The ace also homered off Giants pitcher Madison Bumgarner in the NLDS.

JAVIER BAEZ

INFIELD

Following his first full season, Baez stepped up in a big way during the post-season. He homered in the series opener of the NLDS and went 6 for 16 with a .412 on-base percentage in four games. He was then named co-MVP of the NLCS (along with Jon Lester) after plating five runs and playing stellar defense.

THE 2016 CHICAGO CUBS

KRIS BRYANT

THIRD BASE

The reigning National League Rookie of the Year, Bryant made a case for this year's Senior Circuit MVP honors with 39 home runs and a .939 OPS. His OBP through the first two rounds of the postseason was better than .400.

17

TREVOR CAHILL

PITCHER

Cahill missed a month with tendinitis in his knee but still pitched in 50 games. Pitching in relief, he held opponents to just a .201 average while posting a 2.74 ERA, both career lows.

53

AROLDIS CHAPMAN

PITCHER

After joining the Cubs in a midseason trade with the Yankees, the fireballer continued to top 100 mph on the radar gun. He fanned 90 batters in 58 innings this year and notched three saves in the NLDS.

54

CHRIS COGHLAN

UTILITY

Coghlan, who spent the 2014 and '15 seasons with the Cubs, returned to the club in June after a brief stint in Oakland. He posted a .391 on-base percentage in just over 100 at-bats.

8

WILLSON CONTRERAS

CATCHER

A highly touted catching prospect, Contreras received his Big League call-up in June and proceeded to homer in his first at-bat.

40

CARL EDWARDS JR.

PITCHER

The lanky right-hander from South Carolina harnessed his power to average 95 mph with his fastball and boast a 13.0 K/9 rate over 36 relief appearances in his first season.

DEXTER FOWLER

OUTFIELD

The Cubs' leadoff man reached base at a career-high .393 clip this season thanks to a patient plate approach that yielded 79 free passes. He continued that trend in the postseason, during which he scored six times in the NLCS.

24

JUSTIN GRIMM

PITCHER

Grimm did some of his best work in tight games, posting a 2.12 ERA and holding batters to just a .161 average in 17 such innings in relief.

52

THE 2016 CHICAGO CUBS

JASON HAMMEL

PITCHER

Hammel was one of four members of the Cubs starting staff to win at least 15 games this season, a career high for the 11-year veteran. Ten of those victories came at Wrigley Field, where he held opponents to a .191 average.

39

KYLE HENDRICKS

PITCHER

Hendricks was lights out in his third Big League season, leading all of MLB in ERA (2.13) and ranking second in WHIP (0.98) to contend for the NL Cy Young Award. He fired 7.1 innings of two-hit ball in Game 6 of the NLCS to help the Cubs clinch a World Series berth.

28

THE 2016 CHICAGO CUBS

JASON HEYWARD

OUTFIELD

Heyward, who's played in October in five of the last seven years, scored the winning run of the NLDS-clinching game against the Giants to send the Cubs to their second straight NLCS.

22

MUNENORI KAWASAKI

INFIELD

The effervescent Kawasaki saw limited playing time in his first season in the National League, but he made his opportunities count. Sixteen of his 21 at-bats came in September, when he got on base at a .450 clip to help Chicago secure the NL Central title.

66

TOMMY LA STELLA

THIRD BASE

The 27-year-old La Stella did much of his work this season as a pinch-hitter and was a reliable one at that, posting career highs in both batting average (.270) and OBP (.357) over just about 150 at-bats.

2

THE 2016 CHICAGO CUBS

JOHN LACKEY

PITCHER

Lackey was yet another member of the Cubs' pitching staff that owned an ERA well below the league average. Batters hit just .218 against him, the lowest mark of his 14-year career.

41

THE 2016 CHICAGO CUBS

JON LESTER

PITCHER

The veteran Lester dominated the competition this season, trailing only Hendricks among MLB starters in ERA, and coming up just three K's shy of 200. He was named co-MVP of the NLCS (along with Javier Baez) after posting a 1.38 ERA over 13 innings.

34

THE 2016 CHICAGO CUBS

MIGUEL MONTERO

CATCHER

Montero split time with Contreras and Ross behind the plate but still made an impact. He was responsible for two walk-off hits this year and also connected for a go-ahead grand slam in Game 1 of the NLCS.

47

MIKE MONTGOMERY

PITCHER

Seattle dealt Montgomery to Chicago in July, and in five starts and 12 relief appearances for the Cubs, he whiffed a batter per inning with a 2.82 ERA, a significantly better mark than the one he posted last season.

38

THE 2016 CHICAGO CUBS

SPENCER PATTON

PITCHER

The right-handed reliever and Illinois native volleyed between Triple-A and the Majors during his first season with the Cubs but still averaged just over a strikeout per inning.

45

THE 2016 CHICAGO CUBS

ANTHONY RIZZO

FIRST BASE

Along with Bryant, Rizzo provided pop from the heart of the Cubs' lineup. He matched his career high in home runs (32) while slugging a personal best at .544. Rizzo would experience a power surge in the NLCS, as he slugged two home runs and posted a 1.010 OPS over six games.

44

THE 2016 CHICAGO CUBS

HECTOR RONDON

PITCHER

After saving 18 games through July, Rondon made way for Chapman's arrival at the deadline without hesitation and assumed a set-up role. He owned a paltry 0.98 WHIP on the season.

56

DAVID ROSS

CATCHER

Ross, who won a title with Boston in 2013, averaged a home run in every 17 at-bats this season and launched a longball in the NLDS clincher against the Giants to finish his 15-year career with a bang.

3

ADDISON RUSSELL

SHORTSTOP

At just 22, Russell has already played in a pair of postseasons. The shortstop upped his power in his second campaign, and proved it with two homers against the Dodgers in the NLCS. He also ranked second in MLB in defensive WAR on the season.

27

KYLE SCHWARBER

DESIGNATED HITTER

Schwarber was a late addition to the World Series roster, as the slugger missed all but two games of the season after tearing two ligaments in his knee. Once his health improved, though, the Cubs craved his potent bat, especially since the now-23-year-old launched five longballs last October to become the franchise's all-time postseason home run leader.

12

THE 2016 CHICAGO CUBS

JOE SMITH

PITCHER

Smith debuted in the National League almost a decade ago and, after stints with the Indians and Angels, returned to the Senior Circuit at the trade deadline. He pitched 14.1 innings for Chicago, 9.2 of them in September, when he posted a paltry 0.65 WHIP.

30

JORGE SOLER

OUTFIELD

The Cuba native, who blasted three longballs during the Cubs' 2015 post-season run, hit more home runs and recorded fewer strikeouts than last season despite experiencing a decrease in at-bats.

68

THE 2016 CHICAGO CUBS

PEDRO STROP

PITCHER

In his third full season on the North Side, Strop employed a lethal slider to post his best K/9 rate (11.41) since his debut campaign, all while decreasing his walk rate.

46

MATT SZCZUR

OUTFIELD

The Cubs drafted Szczur out of Villanova in 2010 and he debuted in Chicago four seasons later. This year, he appeared in 100-plus games and got on base at a clip above .300 for the first time in his budding career.

20

TRAVIS WOOD

PITCHER

Wood didn't just help his team's chances from the mound this October. The reliever homered in Game 2 of the NLDS and threw 1.1 innings in relief to usher the Cubs to a 5–2 victory.

37

ROB ZASTRYZNY

PITCHER

The 24-year-old Zastryzny debuted in mid-August and averaged two innings per game in relief down the stretch. He retired more than one-quarter of the batters he faced via strikeout.

29

THE 2016 CHICAGO CUBS

BEN ZOBRIST

UTILITY

A year after winning a ring in Kansas City, 2016 World Series MVP Zobrist joined the Cubs and utilized his skills all over the diamond while reaching base at a .386 clip, the second-best mark of his career.

18

THE 2016 CHICAGO CUBS

REGULAR-SEASON STATS

NO.	PLAYER	B/T	W	L	ERA	SO	BB	SV	BIRTHDATE	BIRTHPLACE
	PITCHERS									
49	JAKE ARRIETA	R/R	18	8	3.10	190	76	0	3/6/86	Farmington, MO
53	TREVOR CAHILL	R/R	4	4	2.74	66	35	0	3/1/88	Oceanside, CA
54	AROLDIS CHAPMAN	L/L	1	1	1.01	46	10	16	2/28/88	Holguin, Cuba
6	CARL EDWARDS JR.	R/R	0	1	3.75	52	14	2	9/3/91	Newberry, SC
52	JUSTIN GRIMM	R/R	2	1	4.10	65	23	0	8/16/88	Bristol, TN
39	JASON HAMMEL	R/R	15	10	3.83	144	53	0	9/2/82	Greenville, SC
28	KYLE HENDRICKS	R/R	16	8	2.13	170	44	0	12/7/89	Newport Beach, CA
41	JOHN LACKEY	R/R	11	8	3.35	180	53	0	10/23/78	Abilene, TX
34	JON LESTER	L/L	19	5	2.44	197	52	0	1/7/84	Tacoma, WA
38	MIKE MONTGOMERY	L/L	1	1	2.82	38	20	0	7/1/89	Mission Hills, CA
45	SPENCER PATTON	R/R	1	1	5.48	22	14	0	2/20/88	Urbana, IL
56	HECTOR RONDON	R/R	2	3	3.53	58	8	18	2/26/88	Guatire, Venezuela
30	JOE SMITH	R/R	1	1	2.51	15	5	0	3/22/84	Cincinnati, OH
46	PEDRO STROP	R/R	2	2	2.85	60	15	0	6/13/85	San Cristobal, D.R
37	TRAVIS WOOD	R/L	4	0	2.95	47	24	0	2/6/87	Little Rock, AR
29	ROB ZASTRYZNY	R/L	1	0	1.13	17	5	0	3/26/92	Corpus Christi, TX

NO.	PLAYER	B/T	AB	H	AVG	HR	RBI	OBP	BIRTHDATE	BIRTHPLACE
	CATCHERS									
40	WILLSON CONTRERAS	R/R	252	71	.282	12	35	.357	5/13/92	Puerto Cabello, Venezuela
47	MIGUEL MONTERO	L/R	241	52	.216	8	33	.327	7/9/83	Caracas, Venezuela
3	DAVID ROSS	R/R	166	38	.229	10	32	.338	3/19/77	Bainbridge, GA
	INFIELDERS									
9	JAVIER BAEZ	R/R	421	115	.273	14	59	.314	12/1/92	Bayamon, Puerto Rico
17	KRIS BRYANT	R/R	603	176	.292	39	102	.385	1/4/92	Las Vegas, NV
66	MUNENORI KAWASAKI	L/R	21	7	.333	0	1	.462	6/3/81	Kagoshima, Japan
2	TOMMY LA STELLA	L/R	148	40	.270	2	11	.357	1/31/89	Westwood, NJ
44	ANTHONY RIZZO	L/L	583	170	.292	32	109	.385	8/8/89	Fort Lauderdale, FL
27	ADDISON RUSSELL	R/R	525	125	.238	21	95	.321	1/23/94	Pensacola, FL
18	BEN ZOBRIST	S/R	523	142	.272	18	76	.386	5/26/81	Eureka, IL
	OUTFIELDERS									
5	ALBERT ALMORA JR.	R/R	112	31	.277	3	14	.308	4/16/94	Hialeah, FL
8	CHRIS COGHLAN	L/R	103	26	.252	1	16	.391	6/18/85	Rockville, MD
24	DEXTER FOWLER	S/R	456	126	.276	13	48	.393	3/22/86	Atlanta, GA
22	JASON HEYWARD	L/L	530	122	.230	7	49	.306	8/9/89	Ridgewood, NJ
12	KYLE SCHWARBER	L/R	4	0	.000	0	0	.200	3/5/93	Middletown, OH
68	JORGE SOLER	R/R	227	54	.238	12	31	.333	2/25/92	Havana, Cuba
20	MATT SZCZUR	R/R	185	48	.259	5	24	.312	7/20/89	Cape May, NJ

Manager: Joe Maddon (70). **Coaches:** Mike Borzello (58), Chris Bosio (25), Brandon Hyde (16), Gary Jones (1), John Mallee (11), Dave Martinez (4), Lester Strode (35)

REGULAR-SEASON RESULTS

MONTH-BY-MONTH RECORD

APRIL
17-5

MAY
18-10

JUNE
16-12

JULY
12-14

AUGUST
22-6

SEPTEMBER
17-10

OCTOBER
1-1

2016 RECORD
103-58

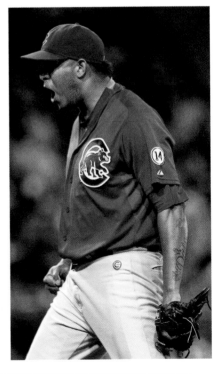

CLOCKWISE FROM BOTTOM LEFT: THE CUBS TOOK THE FIELD ON OPENING DAY WITH HIGH EXPECTATIONS, AND MANAGED TO LIVE UP TO THEM. YOUNG STUD JAVIER BAEZ HIT A WALK-OFF HOMER ON MOTHER'S DAY, MATT SZCZUR PROVIDED VALUE IN HIS FIRST SEASON OF 100-PLUS GAMES, AND HECTOR RONDON NOTCHED 18 SAVES TO HELP THE CLUB CLINCH THE NL CENTRAL.

108 YEARS
IN THE WAIT

The Cubs amassed quite an epic history since the last time they won the World Series.

The autumn of 1908 brought with it the first rematch in the young history of baseball's World Series. The National League's Chicago Cubs, winners of the 1907 campaign, squared off against Ty Cobb and the American League champion Detroit Tigers for the second straight year.

After the Cubs defeated the Tigers in five games in 1907, fans were hoping for a more competitive Fall Classic. But Chicago, led by two victories apiece from pitchers Mordecai Brown and Orval Overall, dispatched of the Tigers in five games again to become the first club ever to win multiple Series. (Granted, the Fall Classic had begun just five years earlier.)

Led by four Hall of Famers, the Cubs appeared destined for more success after their 1908 triumph. But unbeknownst to Chicago's players and fans at the time, that Series was the last taste of a championship the franchise would experience for more than a century. Here are 108 of the most memorable moments in Cubs history since their last World Series championship in 1908.

10.6.1909 On the final day of the season, the Cubs sweep a doubleheader against the Cardinals to finish with 104 wins, but Pittsburgh wins 110 and the NL pennant.

6.28.1910 The Cubs' Joe Tinker ties an MLB record by stealing home twice in one game.

7.12.1910 Franklin Pierce Adams' poem "Baseball's Sad Lexicon" is published in the *New York Evening Mail*, ruing the Cubs' famous double-play combo of Tinker to Evers to Chance.

10.23.1910 Mordecai Brown gives up five runs in the eighth inning of Game 5 of the World Series, as the Philadelphia A's win, 7-2, to claim the championship.

7.17.1918 Both teams use only one pitcher in 21 innings, as Chicago's Lefty Tyler (21 IP, one unearned run) outduels Philadelphia's Milt Watson (20 IP, two earned runs) for the win.

8.1.1918 Hippo Vaughn throws his second one-hit shutout of the season. He goes on to win the unofficial pitching Triple Crown, leading the NL in wins (22), ERA (1.74) and K's (148).

9.11.1918 World War I caused MLB to hold the World Series early. The Cubs lose Game 6 at Fenway Park, becoming the last team to fall to the Red Sox until 2004.

5.30.1927 Cubs shortstop Jimmy Cooney turns what is still one of only seven unassisted triple plays in NL history.

10.6.1912 Heinie Zimmerman finishes by far the best season of his career, leading the NL in average (.372), homers (14) and RBI (104). Although RBI wasn't yet named an official stat, researchers have determined that he should be deemed a Triple Crown winner.

8.31.1915 Cubs right-hander Jimmy Lavender twirls a no-hitter against the Giants at the Polo Grounds with one walk and eight K's.

4.20.1916 The Cubs play their first game at Wrigley Field. Then known as Weeghman Park, it housed the Federal League's Whales from 1914-15.

5.2.1917 Pitchers Hippo Vaughn (Cubs) and Fred Toney (Reds) both throw nine no-hit innings at Weeghman in an impressive pitching duel. But in the 10th inning, Vaughn allows two hits and an unearned run against Cincinnati while Toney completes his no-no.

8.27.1929 The Cubs beat the Reds, 4-1, capping a 47-14 (.770) stretch that takes them from a 2.5-game deficit to a 14.5-game lead in the NL. Chicago ultimately wins its first pennant since 1918.

9.29.1929 Rogers Hornsby goes 4 for 4 with a home run, part of a season-ending 36-game stretch in which he bats .463 with 11 homers and 40 RBI. In his first season with Chicago, the future Hall of Famer sets still-standing team records in average (.380) and hits (229), and wins NL MVP honors.

10.12.1929 The Cubs take an 8-0 lead over the Philadelphia A's in Game 4 of the World Series but fall victim to the biggest comeback in Series history: a 10-run inning against four different pitchers.

9.28.1930 Hack Wilson goes 2 for 3 with two RBI on the final day of the season, bringing his RBI total to 191. That number hasn't been matched in the 86 years since.

FROM LEFT: SCOREBOARD OPERATORS AT WRIGLEY STILL CHANGE THE NUMBERS MANUALLY; THE CUBS WON THE NATIONAL LEAGUE DIVISION SERIES IN 2015 FOR THE FIRST TIME IN MORE THAN A DECADE, BUT THEY LAST REACHED THE WORLD SERIES IN 1945; WRIGLEY FIELD'S UNIQUE FEATURES HAVE WITHSTOOD THE TEST OF TIME, FROM THE SCOREBOARD AND THE BLEACHERS IN THE OUTFIELD TO THE IVY ON THE WALLS.

108 YEARS IN THE WAIT

10.1.1932 In the fifth inning of Game 3 of the World Series at Wrigley Field, Babe Ruth supposedly calls his shot before homering to center.

9.27.1935 The Cubs sweep a doubleheader in St. Louis, capping a 21-game wins streak, still a record, to clinch the National League pennant.

10.7.1935 Facing elimination in Game 6 of the Fall Classic, the Cubs surrender a Series-winning single to the Tigers' Goose Goslin.

9.27.1936 Hall of Famer Billy Herman hits 57 doubles, becoming the only player since 1901 with two such seasons.

9.13.1942 The Cubs win despite committing seven errors, and a record four in one inning by shortstop Lennie Merullo.

8.5.1945 Phil Cavarretta collects his second five-hit, five-RBI game of the season, on his way to a .355 average. No qualified Cubs hitter has matched the mark since.

10.6.1945 Bill Sianis, owner of Chicago's Billy Goat Tavern, and his pet are kicked out of Game 4 of the World Series due to the goat's odor. Sianis says the Cubs will never win another title, and "The Curse of the Billy Goat" begins.

6.11.1952 Cubs left fielder Hank Sauer smacks three solo shots in a 3-2 win.

   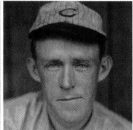 

1937 Hall-of-Fame executive Bill Veeck plants Wrigley's famous ivy. The center-field scoreboard and bleachers are also constructed.

9.28.1938 In nearly complete darkness at Wrigley Field, future Hall of Famer Gabby Hartnett launches an 0-2 curveball for a walk-off longball dubbed "The Homer in the Gloamin.'"

10.6.1938 Cubs starter Dizzy Dean surrenders a go-ahead, two-run homer to the Yankees' Frankie Crosetti in Game 2 of the Fall Classic. New York notches the win and, ultimately, the sweep.

4.26.1941 The Cubs become the first MLB team to liven up a game with organ music.

8.9.1942 In the opening contest of a doubleheader in Cincinnati, which lasted 18 innings, Stan Hack goes 5 for 5 with four walks and a sac bunt. No player since has reached base safely nine times in one game.

9.28.1952 Going into the last game of the season, Cubs outfielder Frank Baumholtz trails only Cardinals outfielder Stan Musial for the NL batting title. In the first, Stan the Man comes in to pitch for the only time in his Hall-of-Fame career. Baumholtz grounds to third, reaching on an error but lowering his average. Musial returns to center and claims the sixth of his seven batting crowns.

9.17.1953 Soon after purchasing his contract from the Negro Leagues' Kansas City Monarchs, the Cubs welcome a 22-year-old Ernie Banks to Wrigley Field.

5.12.1955 The Cubs' Sam Jones becomes the first African-American in MLB history to throw a no-hitter, despite walking seven.

9.19.1955 Shortstop Ernie Banks sets a Big League record (since surpassed) when he hits his fifth grand slam of the season.

4.24.1957 Cubs pitchers Moe Drabowsky, Jackie Collum and

FROM LEFT: CHANCE AND EVERS (SECOND FROM RIGHT) FORMED TWO-THIRDS OF THE CUBS' FAMOUS DOUBLE PLAY TRIO TINKER TO EVERS TO CHANCE; CHARLES WEEGHMAN FOUNDED THE CHICAGO WHALES AND MOVED THEM INTO WEEGHMAN PARK, WHICH WOULD LATER BECOME KNOWN AS WRIGLEY FIELD; ARRIETA THREW A NO-HITTER AGAINST THE DODGERS IN 2015 BEFORE AUTHORING HIS SECOND JUST EIGHT MONTHS LATER.

Jim Brosnan set an unfortunate NL record by combining to walk nine Reds in one inning.

5.13.1958 Moe Drabowsky surrenders a double to Cardinals icon Stan Musial for his 3,000th career hit.

8.21.1958 Ernie Banks smacks his 45th homer, breaking his own single-season record for shortstops. He finishes with 47.

1959 Ernie Banks becomes the first player to win consecutive NL MVP Awards.

5.15.1960 Two days after he's acquired from Philadelphia, Don Cardwell no-hits the Cardinals at Wrigley.

9.9.1965 Dodgers left-hander Sandy Koufax twirls the second NL perfect game of the 20th century, against Chicago.

7.17.1966 Billy Williams singles in his first at-bat at Busch Stadium, doubles in his second, triples in his third and homers in his fourth, becoming the fourth NL player in history to hit for a "natural cycle."

8.19.1969 Ken Holtzman tosses the first of two no-hitters with the Cubs. He becomes one of just two pitchers since 1913 to fail to strike out a single batter in his no-no.

9.9.1969 A black cat runs in front of the visitors' dugout at Shea Stadium, and the Cubs, who had led the NL East by nine

6.26.1960 Four months after his 20th birthday, Ron Santo makes his MLB debut and notches five RBI in a doubleheader.

4.11.1961 In an effort to help his team post its first winning season since 1946, Cubs Owner Philip Wrigley devises the "College of Coaches," rotating them through various roles, including head coach. The Cubs go 64-90 under the direction of four separate skippers.

7.16.1961 A day after his 23rd birthday, Billy Williams hits a grand slam and draws three walks to help the Cubs to a 12-6 win over the Giants. The future Hall of Famer becomes the Cubs' first Rookie of the Year.

6.15.1964 To headline a disastrous six-player trade, the Cubs send Lou Brock to the rival Cardinals for Ernie Broglio. Brock finished his Hall-of-Fame career with 3,023 hits and a then-modern-record 938 steals, while Broglio had a 5.40 ERA in Chicago.

games in mid-August, lose to the Mets, 7-1. After the game, the team goes on a skid and finishes eight games behind New York in the division.

5.12.1970 Ernie Banks goes deep at Wrigley Field for his 500th career home run. He becomes the ninth player to join the prestigious club.

9.30.1971 Fergie Jenkins makes his 39th and final start of the season, and throws his fourth straight complete game on his way to becoming the Cubs' first Cy Young Award winner.

4.16.1972 A 22-year-old Burt Hooton becomes the seventh NL rookie to toss a no-hitter when he blanks the Phillies in just his fourth career start, despite walking seven.

9.2.1972 Righty Milt Pappas comes within one strike of throwing a perfect game before walking pinch-hitter Larry Stahl. He settles for a no-hitter.

FROM LEFT: IN 1998, ROOKIE SENSATION WOOD WHIFFED 20 BATTERS IN JUST HIS FIFTH MAJOR LEAGUE START; BANKS, A SHORTSTOP THAT BOASTED AN UNRIVALVED POWER STROKE AND WELCOMING SMILE, BEGAN HIS HALL-OF-FAME CAREER IN CHICAGO IN 1953 AND WENT ON TO WIN BACK-TO-BACK NATIONAL LEAGUE MVP AWARDS IN 1958 AND '59; VEECK GOT THE IDEA TO PLANT WRIGLEY'S FAMOUS IVY IN 1937.

108 YEARS IN THE WAIT

7.26.1975 Bill Madlock goes 6 for 6 with a triple against the Mets. He hit .354 over the course of the entire season to claim the first of two straight NL batting titles.

4.17.1976 On a wild day at Wrigley, the Cubs take a 13-2 lead, but the Phillies rally to win, 18-16, in extras. Philadelphia's Mike Schmidt becomes the fifth player in modern NL history to homer four times in a game.

6.14.1978 Cubs pitcher Dave Roberts gives up a pair of singles to the Reds' Pete Rose, who begins a 44-game hitting streak, the second longest in modern history.

5.17.1979 The Cubs score 22 runs and tally 26 hits against the

Deemed "The Sandberg Game," it catapults the Cubs to national popularity.

9.24.1984 Rick Sutcliffe's complete game helps Chicago clinch the NL East and reach the playoffs for the first time since '45.

10.7.1984 The Cubs lead, 3-0, in Game 5 of the NLCS, but San Diego scores six in the sixth, capped by Tony Gwynn's go-ahead, two-run double, to win at home.

6.12.1985 The Cubs begin a 13-game losing streak, which tied the modern club record.

6.16.1986 Jamie Moyer, a 23-year-old lefty, makes his MLB

Phillies at Wrigley, yet lose by a run. Philadelphia star third baseman Mike Schmidt hits a go-ahead home run in the 10th inning for the win.

1.27.1982 The Cubs trade Ivan DeJesus to the Phillies for Larry Bowa and a 22-year-old named Ryne Sandberg.

4.9.1982 Broadcast legend Harry Caray calls his first game at Wrigley as the "Voice of the Cubs" for WGN.

8.4.1982 In an afternoon tilt, the Mets' Joel Youngblood singles off Fergie Jenkins before being traded to the Expos. After flying to that night's game in Philadelphia, Youngblood singles off Steve Carlton. That's two hits for two different teams in two cities on the same day.

6.23.1984 Playing in NBC's "Game of the Week," Ryne Sandberg hits game-tying homers in both the bottom of the ninth and 10th en route to a 12-11 win over the rival Cardinals.

debut at Wrigley. Nearly 26 years later, in 2012, a 49-year-old Moyer makes his last appearance for the Rockies.

9.3.1986 Two years after the Cubs draft him in the second round, Greg Maddux makes his MLB debut in an 18-inning game and takes a loss.

8.8.1988 Wrigley hosts its first game under the lights. The matchup against the Phillies lasts just 3.5 innings in heavy rain, so its first official night game is completed the next evening.

8.21.1989 Eventual NL Rookie of the Year Jerome Walton snaps a 30-game hitting streak, the franchise's longest since 1900.

10.7.1989 The Cubs squander a 4-3 lead in Game 3 of the NLCS, as the Giants go on to win the contest, then the series.

3.30.1992 The Cubs acquire a 23-year-old Sammy Sosa from the rival White Sox.

FROM LEFT: EPSTEIN LED THE RED SOX TO TWO WORLD CHAMPIONSHIPS BEFORE JOINING THE CUBS IN 2011 AND MAKING SEVERAL KEY ACQUISITIONS TO IMPROVE THE CLUB; WILLIAMS SPENT ALL BUT TWO SEASONS OF HIS HALL-OF-FAME CAREER WITH CHICAGO; SOSA HIT AT LEAST 60 HOME RUNS IN THREE DIFFERENT SEASONS; CARAY SERVED AS THE BELOVED "VOICE OF THE CUBS" FOR NEARLY TWO DECADES, AND SANDBERG HELPED THE CUBS ACHIEVE NATIONAL NOTORIETY.

108 YEARS IN THE WAIT

9.30.1992 Greg Maddux blanks the Pirates, ending the season with 20 wins, a 2.18 ERA and his first NL Cy Young Award.

7.2.1993 Outfielder Sammy Sosa enjoys a 6-for-6 day at the plate at Denver's Mile High Stadium.

10.3.1993 Closer Randy Myers seals a win in his 18th straight game and notches a club-record 53rd save.

4.4.1994 Tuffy Rhodes becomes the only player in franchise history to hit three homers on Opening Day. Despite his contribution, the Cubs still lose to the Mets.

8.18.1995 In the thin air of Coors Field, the Cubs crush the

10.1.1998 The Cubs blow a 1-0 lead over the Braves in the ninth of NLDS Game 2.

3.29.2000 In the first official MLB game outside North America, the Cubs beat the Mets to open the season at the Tokyo Dome.

5.14.2000 Cubs leadoff man Eric Young sets a team record by stealing five bases.

10.2.2001 Sammy Sosa becomes the only player to post three 60-homer seasons.

8.10.2002 Sammy Sosa hits three three-run homers, becoming the first Cub since 1911 to have a nine-RBI game.

Rockies, 26-7, notching the club's highest run total in a game since 1922.

4.20.1997 The Cubs end their NL-record 14-game losing streak to open a season.

5.6.1998 Eventual NL Rookie of the Year Kerry Wood strikes out 20 Astros, tying the record for a nine-inning game.

6.30.1998 Sammy Sosa belts his 20th home run in 27 games. No player in MLB history has hit more than 18 in a given month.

9.25.1998 Sosa wallops his 66th home run, but the Cardinals' Mark McGwire hits No. 66 the same day before setting the new single-season record at 70.

9.28.1998 Gary Gaetti's two-run homer and Rod Beck's 51st save help the Cubs beat the Giants in a tiebreaker for the NL Wild Card.

8.29.2002 Mark Bellhorn becomes the first NL player ever to homer from both sides of the plate in the same inning.

4.4.2003 Sammy Sosa joins the 500 home run club with his first longball of the season.

10.5.2003 In the decisive fifth game of the NLDS, Kerry Wood holds the Braves to one run, helping the Cubs win a postseason series for the first time in 95 years.

10.14.2003 In Game 6 of the NLCS, Cubs fan Steve Bartman becomes a scapegoat when he touches a catchable foul ball. Instead of securing the out, Chicago allows eight runs and loses.

8.7.2004 In his first year back with the Cubs since '92, Greg Maddux wins No. 300.

9.27.2005 Derrek Lee smacks his NL-leading 50th double of the season.

FROM LEFT: MADDUX BEGAN HIS CAREER IN CHICAGO, WHERE HE WON HIS FIRST OF FOUR STRAIGHT CY YOUNG AWARDS AND WOULD LATER RETURN; WRIGLEY FIELD, A BASTION OF DAYTIME BASEBALL, WAS THE LAST MAJOR LEAGUE STADIUM TO INSTALL LIGHTS, HOSTING ITS FIRST NIGHT GAME IN 1988; ZAMBRANO COLLECTED 125 WINS OVER 11 SEASONS WITH THE CUBS; BARTMAN TOOK THE FALL FOR THE CUBS' LOSS IN THE 2003 NLCS.

108 YEARS IN THE WAIT

8.10.2006 Right-hander Mark Prior makes his final start. Injuries plagued the No. 2 overall pick in the 2001 Draft, and he flamed out at just 25 years old.

9.28.2007 The Cubs beat the Reds to clinch the NL Central with just 84 wins.

10.3.2007 With Game 1 of the NLDS tied, 1–1, Manager Lou Piniella pulls Carlos Zambrano for Carlos Marmol. He gives up two runs to Arizona, who goes on to sweep.

9.14.2008 Carlos Zambrano throws a no-hitter against the Astros — in Milwaukee. The game was moved from Houston due to Hurricane Ike.

6.6.2013 With the No. 2 pick of the 2013 Draft, the Cubs select Kris Bryant from the University of San Diego.

7.2.2013 In the midst of a 96-loss season, the Cubs trade Scott Feldman to Baltimore for Jake Arrieta, who had a 5.46 career ERA.

12.13.2014 The Cubs announce that they have signed free-agent pitcher Jon Lester to a six-year, $155-million deal.

8.15.2015 The Cubs topple the White Sox for their 15th win in 16 games on the way to 97 victories on the season.

10.7.2015 Jake Arrieta strikes out 11 Pirates and records a shutout in the NL Wild Card Game.

9.20.2008 The Cubs beat the Cardinals to clinch the NL Central on their way to 97 wins. For the first time since 1906–08, they reach the postseason in consecutive years.

10.1.2008 The Dodgers' James Loney hits a grand slam in Game 1 of the NLDS, erasing the Cubs' only lead of the series.

5.27.2009 Carlos Zambrano takes out his frustrations on a Gatorade dispenser when a call doesn't go in his favor and is suspended for six games.

8.6.2011 Carlos Zambrano hits his 23rd Cubs home run. He retires with 24, eight more than any other pitcher since 1970.

10.25.2011 The Cubs introduce Theo Epstein as the team's new president of baseball operations.

1.6.2012 Chicago sends Andrew Cashner to San Diego for Anthony Rizzo, who had hit .141 in his first taste of MLB in '11.

10.13.2015 Anthony Rizzo's sixth-inning solo homer provides the go-ahead run in Game 4 of the NLDS, capping Chicago's first victory in a postseason series (Wild Card excluded) since '03.

10.20.2015 In Game 3 of the NLCS, the Cubs enter the sixth in a 2–2 tie before the Mets score the go-ahead run on a wild pitch. New York takes the game and sweeps the series.

4.21.2016 After no-hitting the Dodgers in August 2015, Jake Arrieta does the same to the Reds just nine regular-season starts later — the third-shortest gap in Major League history.

5.8.2016 The Cubs walk Bryce Harper six times (three intentionally) and hit him once, making him the first modern-era player to go to the plate seven times without recording an at-bat.

6.27.2016 Kris Bryant goes 5 for 5 against the Reds, becoming the first player since 1913 to collect at least three home runs and two doubles in a game.

FROM LEFT: WRIGLEY'S IVY LOSES SOME OF ITS GREEN IN THE FALL, AND FANS KNOW THEY'RE LUCKY ENOUGH TO BE EXPERIENCING POSTSEASON BASEBALL WHEN THEY SEE IT CHANGE HUE; UNTIL THIS YEAR, THE LAST TIME THE CUBS REACHED THE WORLD SERIES WAS IN 1945, WHEN THEY LOST TO THE TIGERS IN SEVEN GAMES; BRYANT, THE CUBS' FIRST SELECTION IN THE 2013 DRAFT, WON THE NL ROOKIE OF THE YEAR AWARD IN 2015 AND FOLLOWED THE ACCOMPLISHMENT WITH AN MVP-WORTHY CAMPAIGN IN HIS SOPHOMORE SEASON.

CHICAGO CUBS
2016 MINOR LEAGUE RESULTS

AAA IOWA CUBS (67-76)
3rd in Pacific Coast League American–North Division

AA TENNESSEE SMOKIES (58-81)
4th in Southern League North Division

HIGH-A MYRTLE BEACH PELICANS (82-57)
2nd in Carolina League Southern Division

CLASS-A SOUTH BEND CUBS (84-55)
2nd in Midwest League Eastern Division

SHORT-SEASON A EUGENE EMERALDS (54-22)
1st in Northwest League South Division

ARIZONA LEAGUE CUBS (28-28)
4th in Arizona League East Division

ONCE IN A LIFETIME

Superstars like Kris Bryant don't come around often.

The past two seasons have been a whirlwind for Cubs superstar Kris Bryant. He's just 24, but in the span of 18 months, he has made his MLB debut, played in two All-Star Games, compiled a pair of 25-plus–home run seasons, carried Chicago to the playoffs twice and won the 2015 NL Rookie of the Year Award. Oh, and did we mention that during all this, he got engaged to his high school sweetheart and went swimming with sharks?

Now, with his second full campaign behind him, Bryant has also claimed the ultimate prize: a World Series ring. As he looked back on his championship-winning sophomore season in Chicago, the Cubs' slugger spoke about his towering expectations.

The Cubs are a very young club, and it seems as though you guys have a lot of fun together. How would you describe the team dynamic?
A lot of us are pretty close to each other in age and we relate to each other on that level, so we have fun here on a daily basis. We bring DJs and animals to the field and really get to experience the fun of baseball being on the Chicago Cubs.

What's your take on playing for a quirky manager like Joe Maddon?
Everybody should do it. I think the game is shifting a little bit to having more fun and not taking things so seriously during times like [Spring Training]. Obviously on the field, you take it very seriously. But Joe is just a trip. He's so much fun to play for and he keeps it light in the clubhouse. I've enjoyed my time with him so far.

How did it feel to win the National League Rookie of the Year Award last fall?
Winning that award was a huge honor. There are a lot of guys, even around this clubhouse, who were very deserving. You only get one year to win it, and I had a lot of good competition. It was definitely one of my favorite things so far in my baseball career.

ONCE IN A LIFETIME

After that you had quite an exciting offseason, too.
I couldn't have written it better myself. Having an unbelievable year, both individually and as a team, and then in the offseason getting engaged, going to Hawaii and swimming with sharks, I just really enjoyed it.

What made you decide to go swimming with sharks?
We were like, "Why not do it? We're in Hawaii." I guess like, "When in Rome, do as the Romans."

I get terribly seasick when I'm on a boat, but I just thought, "I have to do this and say I swam with sharks." It's once-in-a-lifetime.

I was underwater in the cage for 20 minutes — just enough time to get sick. I'm never going to do it again, but it was fun.

Do you know what kind of sharks they were?
They were Galapagos sharks and sand sharks. No great whites or tiger sharks. They said those are the scary ones.

Does that mean you're a pretty adventurous guy in general?
I don't know if I'd say I am. I'm slowly getting to that point. A couple years ago, you couldn't have gotten me in the water with sharks. But I'm realizing that there are a lot of opportunities coming my way to do cool things like that, and you've got to be crazy not to take advantage of them.

After such a huge rookie showing, what were your expectations for this season?
I just really looked at this year as a continuation of last year, with a little break in the middle for the offseason. Just trying to build upon things, as a team and individually.

The vibe that I got from everybody was that our expectations were bigger than anybody else's out there. We expected a lot out of ourselves, and we held each other accountable. We heard a lot of the speculation, but as professionals, our own expectations were through the roof.

How did it feel to be named an NL All-Star during your first season in 2015?
That was so much fun, especially having my whole family there and having my dad throw to me during the Home Run Derby. At the time, I was just in awe. I was competing against Albert Pujols. Ken Griffey Jr. was there.

To do it in my first year was a once-in-a-lifetime thing. I'll remember it for a very long time. Four years ago, I never would have thought I would do that. It was an unbelievable experience.

What was it like to be among so many of your teammates on the 2016 NL All-Star team?
It makes the whole All-Star experience a lot more fun. I'm not saying last year wasn't fun, but having that many people to share it with made it even better. You don't really see it that often. It was very exciting. Guys were playing extremely well and everything was clicking.

Do you try to emulate any of your peers?
Most recently, Evan Longoria. He's a very underrated player, but he's one of the best third basemen in the game. I can learn a lot from watching him, defensively and at the plate.

You played with Bryce Harper as a kid. What do you remember from those days?
I played with him when I was around 8 or 9 years old and then again when we were 13 and 14. All I really remember was just how much better he was than anybody on the field. He was leaps above everybody. He would get up to the plate and hit bombs. At that time, I knew the type of player he would be, and he won the National League MVP. I kind of expected that.

You certainly had an MVP-worthy campaign yourself.
Typically I don't set goals around awards, but I think if I do things the right way and focus on the team and helping us win — I've always done it that way — things will turn out for the better. So I'll just continue doing that and see where things go.

Do you pay much attention to stats?
I try not to look at stats. I did that so much in high school, and it can really cloud your vision. You can't focus on the numbers; they're always changing.

My dad has always said, "You are who you are as a player, and you're going to end up where you're meant to at the end of the year." And he's always right.

Your performance this year earned you and David Ortiz the 2016 Hank Aaron Award, given during the World Series to the most outstanding offensive performer in each league. Can you describe that honor?
It was truly an honor to be up there with two of the best baseball players to ever play this game. I've been through some pretty cool things recently, but this is something I'm going to have to pinch myself for. Obviously David Ortiz had an unbelievable career, and he's going out as I'm just making my way in. One of the best baseball players that ever lived was sitting next to me. It was such a surreal moment.

"I'm realizing that there are a lot of opportunities coming my way to do cool things, and you've got to be crazy not to take advantage of them."

A DECADE OF CHAMPIONS

Unprecedented parity during the last 10 years of Major League Baseball has ushered 11 different ballclubs into the World Series. Of those teams, six have come out on top.

ECKSTEIN WON THE 2006 WORLD SERIES MVP AWARD AFTER HITTING .364 IN ST. LOUIS'S FIVE-GAME WIN OVER THE TIGERS.

2006

ST. LOUIS CARDINALS

From 2000–05, the Cardinals had reached the playoffs in all but one year, advanced to the NLCS three times, and competed for one World Series title. But until 2006, they hadn't actually won it all since way back in 1982.

Despite finishing with nearly 20 fewer regular-season victories than they had in the previous two seasons (the club went 105-57 in 2004 and 100-62 in '05), the Cardinals put it all together against Detroit in 2006. Twice in the five-game Series, St. Louis defeated the Tigers' Justin Verlander, including in Game 1, when the visiting club sent Verlander to the showers after he surrendered six runs in five innings. Albert Pujols and Scott Rolen each contributed to the Cardinals' offensive onslaught, slugging a home run apiece.

Although St. Louis would not go yard for the rest of the Series, the entire lineup played a role in the victory. In fact, light-hitting infielder David Eckstein, who helped the Angels to a title four years prior, proved to be the star, earning Series MVP honors on the heels of an eight-hit, three-run, four-RBI performance. Detroit showed some life at home in Game 2, which they won, 3-1, but the Cardinals ultimately outscored the Tigers, 22-11, over the course of the Series to clinch their first title in more than two decades at Busch Stadium.

WORLD SERIES MVP LOWELL BATTED .400 WITH A HOME RUN AND FOUR RBI IN BOSTON'S FOUR-GAME SWEEP OF COLORADO. IT WAS THE RED SOX'S SECOND CHAMPIONSHIP IN FOUR SEASONS FOLLOWING AN 86-YEAR TITLE DROUGHT.

2007

BOSTON RED SOX

Some moments in time, although it may not be obvious as they happen, can carry great symbolic weight. In 2007, the Red Sox's Mike Lowell had enjoyed one of his most successful campaigns. What best served to endear him to fans forever, though, was a magnificent performance in that year's World Series.

Lowell, who in 1999 had battled testicular cancer as a member of the Marlins, willed the Red Sox's offense to overcome the Colorado Rockies and finish off a Series sweep. Boston's bats chased Rockies starting pitcher Jeff Francis early in Game 1 while romping to a 13-1 victory. Game 2 was a tighter, 2-1 affair, but the Sox still prevailed at home. When the Series flipped to Coors Field, the visitors rolled again, taking a commanding, 3-games-to-none lead.

In the seventh inning of Game 4, Lowell padded the Sox's lead with a solo home run off Aaron Cook. The World Series MVP Award winner's blast proved to be the difference-maker.

Hitting fifth in the lineup behind formidable sluggers Manny Ramirez and David Ortiz, it was Lowell who provided most of the offensive thunder throughout the Fall Classic, batting .400 with four extra-base hits — and adding a stolen base for good measure — as Beantown celebrated its second world title in four years.

> **"We're all one big unit that's trying to accomplish the same goal. But there's more than just the nine guys on the field, and I think you have to give credit to a lot of people."**
>
> *Mike Lowell*

A DECADE OF CHAMPIONS

2008

PHILADELPHIA PHILLIES

The 2008 Series was a study in contrasts. While the Phillies' front office proved it was willing to invest heavily in the future, the Rays epitomized a small-market club. Philadelphia had history and a World Series title under its belt; Tampa Bay, meanwhile, had never finished better than fourth place in the AL East, and that happened only once in its first decade of existence. And as comfortable as the mid-70-degree nights were when the Series opened at Tropicana Field, things were equally miserable at Citizens Bank Park, as temperatures plunged to the mid-40s and monsoon-like conditions postponed play. At one point, Commissioner Bud Selig even declared, "We'll celebrate [Thanksgiving] here if we have to."

Thankfully, it didn't quite come to that. Instead, 2006 National League MVP Ryan Howard knocked three homers for the victorious club, while veterans Jimmy Rollins, Carlos Ruiz, Shane Victorino and Jayson Werth joined him to provide all the pop the offense needed to stay on top. The Phillies' bats were especially potent in Game 4, knocking 10 runs against a foursome of Rays pitchers.

Philadelphia's staff, on the other hand, featured farm system product Cole Hamels, who combined with Joe Blanton and J.C. Romero to collect all four Fall Classic wins while limiting the Rays to just one. When closer Brad Lidge locked down his second save in the clinching Game 5, he brought fans along with him to their knees.

LIDGE CELEBRATED WITH RUIZ ON THE FIELD AT CITIZENS BANK PARK AFTER NOTCHING THE SAVE IN THE DECIDING GAME 5 OF THE '08 WORLD SERIES.

2009

NEW YORK YANKEES

It was a bold move when new Yankees Manager Joe Girardi donned a No. 27 jersey at the 2007 press conference announcing his hiring. But everyone knew its significance. So it was especially sweet when the man wearing No. 27 joined his charges in celebrating the team's 27th championship just two years later.

The 2009 Yankees were champions because their core of veterans — Derek Jeter, Mariano Rivera, Jorge Posada and Andy Pettitte — meshed perfectly with the reinforcements brought in by GM Brian Cashman and his staff. Pettitte notched two wins and Rivera a pair of saves in the World Series alone. Alex Rodriguez launched six home runs that October. And Series MVP Hideki Matsui posted an otherworldly 2.027 OPS in 13 Fall Classic at-bats.

Those performances helped the Yankees outlast a Phillies team gunning for a dramatic repeat. Despite a historic hitting display by Chase Utley, untouchable curveballs from Cliff Lee and the confidence of having been there a year earlier, the Phillies dropped three straight after winning Game 1, and couldn't recover. After sending the Series back to the Bronx for Game 6, Philadelphians could only watch as Godzilla (as Matsui was affectionately called) trampled their city's title hopes. "When you play in the World Series, someone has to go home," Phillies skipper Charlie Manuel said after Game 6. "All of a sudden you play four out of seven and then lose, and someone tells you to go home."

In the end, it was New York's year. For the 27th time, the Yankees were world champs.

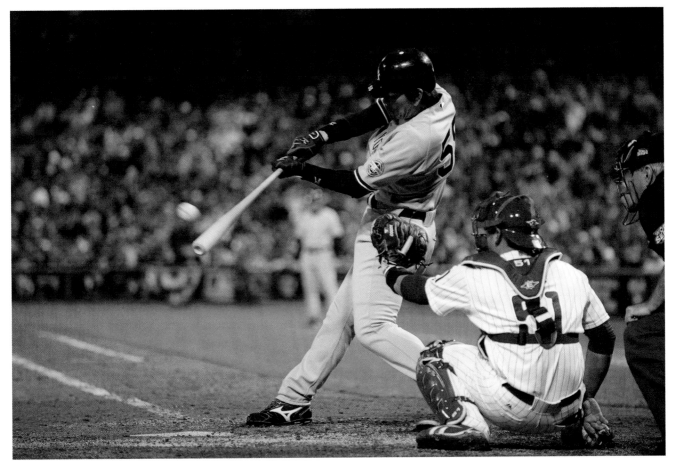

MATSUI POSTED AN INCREDIBLE .615 BATTING AVERAGE AGAINST THE PHILLIES IN THE '09 WORLD SERIES, INCLUDING A 3-FOR-4, SIX-RBI PERFORMANCE IN THE DECISIVE GAME 6.

LINCECUM, WHO GOT A W IN EACH OF THE FIRST TWO ROUNDS OF THE POSTSEASON, WON A PAIR OF 2010 FALL CLASSIC GAMES, INCLUDING GAMES 1 AND 5, THE LATTER OF WHICH WAS A DOMINANT EIGHT-INNING OUTING AGAINST TEXAS.

2010

SAN FRANCISCO GIANTS

Going into the 2010 postseason, it seemed that most of the media's attention was directed away from the dominant staff in San Francisco, led by Tim Lincecum. Instead, the focus was locked on the Phillies' rotation and the Rangers' potent offense. Throughout that postseason, though, the 2008 NL Cy Young Award winner made sure that neither he, nor the rest of the Giants rotation, would be overlooked again.

Lincecum dominated in his first ever playoff start with one of the best games of his already impressive career. He struck out an incredible 14 Braves while allowing just two hits. He then set the tone in the NLCS by beating the Phillies in Game 1, outdueling ace Roy Halladay and striking out eight.

And Lincecum was just as dominant in the World Series, during which he matched up with Rangers ace Cliff Lee, who through that point was 7-0 in the postseason with a microscopic 1.26 ERA. To the delight of fans, the right-hander would face off against Lee a second time in the Series, as well. Lincecum got the better of him in both outings, winning Game 1 and then shoring up the Giants' World Series victory with eight stellar innings in Game 5 to wrap up one of the most overpowering October pitching performances in baseball history.

LA RUSSA BEGAN HIS MANAGERIAL CAREER IN 1979 AND FINISHED IT ON A HIGH NOTE WITH A 2011 WORLD SERIES TITLE, THE THIRD CHAMPIONSHIP OF HIS CAREER.

2011

ST. LOUIS CARDINALS

On August 25, 2011, the Cardinals were nine-and-a-half games behind the first-place Milwaukee Brewers in the NL Central. With five weeks left in the season, their playoff hopes were slim.

At that point, Cardinals Manager Tony La Russa, who was set to retire after the season, gathered his troops. "Play every game like it's the last game of your life," he urged. The mantra worked, as the Cards would finish on a 22-9 run, narrowly securing the Wild Card spot.

After fashioning that comeback, the Cardinals would just keep coming back. They came from behind to top the Phillies in the NLDS before repeating the feat against the Brewers in the NLCS. In Game 6 of the World Series, the Cards trailed the Rangers, 3 games to 2, when NLCS and eventual Series MVP David Freese came to the plate in the ninth with two on and two outs. He tripled, knotting the score and sending the game to extras. Leading off the 11th, Freese came through with the game-winning home run. St. Louis took Game 7, too, after the third baseman hit a two-run double in the first inning.

"It was overwhelming," said La Russa. "We were on the edge game after game after game. [When] you play with that urgency, it's a little scary, but it's really fun to compete that way."

> **"We were on the edge game after game after game. When you play with that urgency, it's a little scary, but it's really fun to compete that way."**
>
> *Cardinals Manager Tony La Russa*

2012

SAN FRANCISCO GIANTS

In 2012, San Francisco was just two years removed from their 2010 title, and two regular-season wins better than that year's postseason contenders. But they were also just one year removed from a season in which they finished eight games out of the playoffs, and needed to neutralize the Tigers and ace Justin Verlander if they were again to achieve glory.

Pablo Sandoval dominated the opening game with a record-tying three-longball performance. Game 2 remained scoreless through six-and-a-half frames, as starters Madison Bumgarner and Doug Fister traded zeroes. But the Giants eventually eked out two runs, and Sergio Romo preserved the victory with a perfect ninth inning. Detroit was again unable to score in Game 3, this time against Ryan Vogelsong, who just two years before had been released from a Minor League contract.

The fearless team sent ace Matt Cain to the hill for Game 4, and jumped on the scoreboard in the second inning. The Tigers roared back, however, when Miguel Cabrera launched a two-run shot to give them their first lead of the entire Series. But the Giants, too, had an MVP candidate in the lineup, and Buster Posey belted a two-run homer of his own to regain the lead for the Giants at 3-2.

A Delmon Young longball in the bottom of the sixth tied the score once more, but NLCS hero Marco Scutaro again came through with a two-out RBI single in extra innings that proved to be the game, and Series, winner.

SANDOVAL WENT DEEP THREE TIMES IN A RECORD-TYING PERFORMANCE IN GAME 1, HELPING TO LEAD THE GIANTS TO THEIR SECOND TITLE IN THREE YEARS.

A DECADE OF CHAMPIONS

UEHARA JUMPED INTO THE ARMS OF DAVID ROSS AFTER RECORDING THE LAST OUT OF THE 2013 WORLD SERIES. BOSTON'S THIRD TITLE IN A DECADE WAS THE FIRST CLINCHED AT FENWAY PARK IN ALMOST 100 YEARS.

2013

BOSTON RED SOX

After finishing last in the AL East in 2012 with a 69-93 record, the Red Sox were faced with the formidable challenge of regaining respect in 2013. Under new skipper John Farrell, they managed to reverse course, finishing with an AL-best 97-65 record. The Cardinals, meanwhile, came just one win shy of the 2012 Series, losing to the eventual champion Giants.

When the teams met in the 2013 Classic, Boston got off to a quick start, scoring five runs in the first two innings off Cards ace Adam Wainwright, leading to an 8-1 win. St. Louis bounced back to capture Games 2 and 3, the latter on an obstruction call, which marked the first time a World Series game ended on such a play. In the bottom of the ninth, with the score level at 4-4, Allen Craig scored the game-winning run after tripping over third baseman Will Middlebrooks.

The Red Sox rebounded to win the next two games before going up against rookie Michael Wacha, who had previously been unbeaten in the playoffs, at home for Game 6. The Boston bats collected three runs each in the third and fourth innings, and when closer Koji Uehara struck out Matt Carpenter to end the game, it sealed the Red Sox's third championship in 10 years and the first title at Fenway Park since 1918.

2014

SAN FRANCISCO GIANTS

The 2014 Fall Classic featured two teams with drastically different recent postseason histories. The Royals hadn't played October baseball since they won it all in 1985. The Giants, meanwhile, were gunning for their third world title in five years, and they would earn that crown thanks to a legendary performance from starting pitcher Madison Bumgarner.

After securing a dominant, 7–1 win in the opener at Kansas City's Kauffman Stadium, Bumgarner returned to the mound again for Game 5 at AT&T Park, where he tossed a shutout in front of a hometown crowd to help the Giants regain the Series advantage. But following a 10–0, Game 6 loss in which San Francisco's bats went silent, Bumgarner stepped up in a big way. The towering southpaw threw five innings of scoreless relief in Game 7 to earn the save and clinch the franchise's eighth World Series title.

"[Bumgarner] is a guy that is able to elevate his game," Buster Posey said. "He's extremely competitive."

The southpaw allowed just one run over 21 innings en route to being named the Series MVP. In the process, he lowered his career Fall Classic ERA to 0.25, the best all-time among pitchers with at least 20 World Series innings of work.

> "[Bumgarner] is a guy that is able to elevate his game. He's extremely competitive."
>
> *Buster Posey*

IN 2014, BUMGARNER WON TWO GAMES AND PICKED UP A FIVE-INNING SAVE IN THE CLINCHING GAME 7, RECORDING ONE OF THE GREATEST PITCHING PERFORMANCES IN WORLD SERIES HISTORY. THE TOWERING SOUTHPAW LOWERED HIS CAREER FALL CLASSIC ERA TO A RECORD 0.25.

2015

KANSAS CITY ROYALS

Salvador Perez and the Royals wanted to make things up to their fanbase after coming up just 90 feet short in the 2014 World Series. From the start of 2015, Kansas City was focused, and the team led its division wire-to-wire on its way to assembling the American League's best record.

In the postseason, the Royals showed grit and determination to make it to the Fall Classic, defeating a young Astros team in a five-game ALDS and holding off Toronto's potent bats in the ALCS. The last obstacle standing in the way of their crown was an upstart New York Mets team that boasted a dominant pitching staff.

Kansas City took Game 1 in 14 innings on an Eric Hosmer sacrifice fly before securing a 7-1 win in Game 2 behind a complete-game two-hitter from Johnny Cueto. After dropping Game 3 on the road, the club capitalized on an error to secure a win in Game 4. And in the Game 5 Series clincher, Kansas City manufactured a come-from-behind victory for the fourth time in the Series. Hosmer scored the game-tying run in the ninth on a ground ball to third and a subsequent wild throw to the plate, and his teammates would score five runs in the 12th inning to take home the title.

"This is just too good of a group, too good of a team, not to be remembered as world champions," Hosmer said after it was all over. "We accomplished a lot last year, but to come back and finish the job, it's unbelievable."

MIKE MOUSTAKAS AND HOSMER CELEBRATED THE ROYALS' CROWNING ACHIEVEMENT FOLLOWING GAME 5 OF THE 2015 WORLD SERIES AT CITI FIELD.

MAJOR LEAGUE BASEBALL

President, Business & Media	Bob Bowman
Executive Vice President, Content; Editor-in-Chief, MLBAM	Dinn Mann
Vice President, Publishing	Donald S. Hintze
Editorial Director	Mike McCormick
Account Executive	Jake Schwartzstein
Managing Editor	Allison Duffy-Davis
Specialist, Content Media	Alex Trautwig
Project Art Director	Melanie Finnern
Project Assistant Editor	Joe Sparacio

MAJOR LEAGUE BASEBALL PHOTOS

Manager	Jessica Carroll
Photo Editor	Jim McKenna

WORLD SERIES CONTRIBUTING PHOTOGRAPHERS

Brad Mangin, LG Patterson, Alex Trautwig,
Rob Tringali, Ron Vesely

PENGUIN RANDOM HOUSE TEAM

President & CEO	Brad Martin
President & Publisher	Kristin Cochrane
VP, Publisher, McClelland & Stewart	Jared Bland
SVP, Director of Production	Janine Laporte
Associate Managing Editor	Kimberlee Hesas
Assistant Manager, Production	Christie Hanson
Executive Sales Director	Scott Loomer
Executive Sales Director	Liza Morrison
Publicity Manager	Ruta Liormonas
Senior Marketing Director	Constance Mackenzie
Typesetter/Design Associate	Erin Cooper
Senior Designer	Five Seventeen
